Japanese Cooking

Contemporary & Traditional

Simple, Delicious, and Vegan

Miyoko Nishimoto Schinner

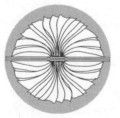

Book Publishing Company
Summertown, Tennessee

Pictured on font cover, clockwise from upper left: Vegetarian Eel Over Rice (Unaju or Unagi Donburi), page 142; Fried Tofu Dumplings (Hirosu), page 81; Daikon Salad with Lime-Ume Dressing (Daikon Salada), page 164

Pictured on back cover, clockwise from lower left: Bottom tray—Fried Tofu Dumplings (Hirosu), page 81; Stewed (Ni-Mono) konnyaku, carrots, lotus root, burdock root, page 128; Upper Box (clockwise form left)—Freeze-Dried Tofu (Koya dofu), page 82; Stewed (Ni-Mono) taro root and bamboo shoots, page 128; Bowl on right—New Year's Stew with O-Mochi (Ozoni), page 69

Published in the United States of America by:

    Book Publishing Co.
    P.O. Box 99
    Summertown, TN 38483
    888-260-8458

02 01 00 99　　　　　6 5 4 3 2 1

ISBN 1-57067-072-2

Schinner, Miyoko Nishimoto,
    Japanese cooking Contemporary & traditional : simple, delicious,
  and vegan / Miyoko Nishimoto Schinner.
        P. Cm.
   Includes index.
   ISBN 1-57067-072-2 (alk. paper)
    1. Vegetarian cookery. 2. Cookery, Japanese. I. Title.
  II. Title. Contemporary and traditional Japanese cooking.
  TX837.S29 1999

                  98-54936
                  CIP

Contents

Introduction
Historical and New Flavors of Japan

Ishi-yaki-imo! Ishi-yaki-imo! The singsong cry of the sweet potato peddler would echo again and again, resounding into every home on the street. Children and mothers, lured by the sweet smell, would run out to buy the simple treat from the hand-pulled cart, heavily laden with sweet potatoes buried in hot rocks. I remember, too, as a young child being lured by the beauty of the cry, warming my hands over the rocks in the cart and biting into the smoky sweetness of roasted yams.

Today, the ubiquitous sweet potato peddler drives a truck and has a recording of his famous cry playing repeatedly over a megaphone. Still, his truck is filled with the same rocks and potatoes; still, the wafting smell is as sweet and smoky. Thirty years later, the satisfaction felt from biting into the steaming hot potato is as uncomplicated and deep, a joy that can only be derived from the simplest things.

Japanese cuisine, as may be said of many things Japanese, is grounded in simplicity and purity. Whereas the cuisine of other cultures may dazzle and delight by the complexity of ingredients and techniques, Japanese cuisine reduces the number of components in a dish to a minimalist act that allows the character of each player to resonate with clarity. Flavors are pure and true, unfettered by the many spices and seasonings encountered in dishes of other countries. A classic example would be *Horenso-no-Hitashi*, where blanched spinach is served with just a sprinkling of soy sauce. The sweetness of the spinach is hardly ever so pronounced as when served in such stark simplicity. Another is *Furo Fuki Daikon* (page 130), a warming dish of thick daikon radish rounds simmered until practically melting, topped with a sweet miso sauce. The delicate flavor of fresh tofu may be accentuated only by a zesty *ponzu* (light, salty, citrus dipping sauce) in *Yu-Dofu* (Tofu in Hot Water). Or with the roasted sweet potatoes the food can stand on its own. How absolutely zen that so much can result from so little!

The ultimate dining experiences in Japan is *kaiseki* cuisine. They take place at country inns, temples, and hundreds-of-years-old restaurants where a diner sits on *tatami* mats in a starkly decorated room. The *shoji* screen doors are flung wide open, and the room spills out into a Japanese garden of elegantly situated rocks, ponds filled with colorful carp, small shrubs, perhaps a crimson maple tree or two—and tranquility. The diner finds spread before him a vast array of comestibles, each displayed with grace in a variety of individual ceramic and porcelain dishes. The utmost care is taken to adorn each dish, whether it be the accent of a tiny leaf resting on one, or the beautiful composition of a few vegetables in another. The meal thus reflects the garden, consisting of numerous components, each pure and simple, the whole harmonizing in a pastoral symphony. I recall the first time I stayed at a *ryokan* (high-class Japanese inn) and was amazed at the splendid display—perhaps twelve to fifteen dishes!—served in the privacy of our own room. Or the leisurely afternoon spent at a temple for nuns in Tottori Prefecture, where we dined for several hours on course after course (each being very small, of course) of truly vegan *shojin-ryori* (Buddhist vegetarian cooking).

Naturally, most of Japan does not dine on a daily basis on such elaborate *kaiseki* cuisine. Although the average Japanese meal served at home would not consist of fifteen dishes, many housewives still prepare five or six. In addition to rice, a typical meal would include soup, either miso or clear, *o-shinko* (pickles), a protein item such as broiled fish or chilled tofu, a couple of vegetable dishes, perhaps one blanched and the other stewed, and a small and soothing salad in rice vinegar.

From Kyushu in the south to Hokkaido in the far north, you will find the same basic dishes—*tempura*, *soba*, and *ni-mono* (stewed dishes)—in addition to regional specialties. They will differ primarily in the degree of seasoning used. In the warm south, people prefer their food to be *usu-aji* (lightly seasoned) with only a splash of soy sauce or a pinch of sea salt. Folks from Hokkaido, or even Tokyo, sometimes find this bland, although natives will attest that it is simply more subtle. In the cold north, *koi aji* (deeper flavor) is favored, and the *dashi* (stock) used is darker, saltier, and richer; folks from Osaka often find it too salty. My mother, the *Edokko* in our family (a person born and raised in the original parts of Tokyo, once called Edo), always prefers her food seasoned with more soy sauce, miso, and salt than I do. (Interestingly, the further north one goes in Japan, the more cases of hypertension one encounters.) In some areas, they may even use a heavy hand in adding sugar. I found that in Tottori Prefecture, a region to the south, the soup stock for udon noodles verged on being strangely sweet. Thus, the amount of soy sauce, miso, sea salt, and sweetener can be varied according to personal taste, and recipes provided in this book often indicate a range.

The Japanese archipelago, once isolated from the world except for the infamous Black Ships from the Netherlands, has eagerly borrowed and absorbed as much from the rest of the world as possible. An exciting culinary evolution has taken place, especially in the past twenty years or so, particularly with the influx of French and Mediterranean cuisine. The influence of the West and other cultures has rendered a new cuisine celebrated by many creative young chefs in Tokyo and other large cities that marry components of two cultures while maintaining traditional Japanese simplicity. This is what I call *Nouveau Japonaise* (Nouvelle Japanese Cuisine). In addition, the past several decades have also fostered the development of a new home-style cooking, which also often marries the flavors of two cultures. These earthy, albeit sometimes not too healthful, dishes seem to be a favorite of children. They come with names such as "Curry Rice," *Korrokeh* (Potato Croquettes), and "White Stew" (a bechamel sauce-based stew with vegetables and, usually, meat). Although neither style of cuisine can boast a tradition as long as *Furo Fuki Daikon* (Stewed Daikon with Sweet Miso, page 130), they have become utterly incorporated into the modern Japanese diet, forever changing the face of the centuries-old shoyu-flavored cuisine. In this book, I have devoted a chapter to each one of these new traditions, vegan-style.

Japanese Attitudes Toward Nutrition and Vegetarianism

Although dietary habits are changing rapidly, the Japanese believe that good health comes from eating small amounts of a wide variety of foods. The Japanese Ministry of Health encourages eating thirty different types of food each day, a guideline that is far more overreaching than the USDA's Food Pyramid. Some of the food groups included would baffle most Westerners, including one for sea vegetables and another for fermented foods, all considered essential to good health. Most Japanese today still consume food from many of these food groups. However, a deterioration in the overall quality of the diet is apparent as many Japanese, especially those in urban areas, depart from a traditional diet. The Japanese, who throughout most of history considered it uncivilized and unclean to kill and eat a four-legged creature, now pride themselves for their $50-per-pound Kobe beef, considering it uncivilized not to consume some animal protein at practically every meal. Dairy products, absent from the Japanese diet for centuries, have in recent years become more prevalent, thanks to a highly intrusive and successful marketing campaign spearheaded by the American dairy industry. Now just about every Japanese school child drinks milk, and every mother believes it is necessary to provide enough calcium in the diet and prevent osteoporosis.

At its worst, the traditional breakfast of rice, *nori* (a toasted sea vegetable), miso soup, and a protein dish has been replaced by inch-thick white bread toast and coffee. Lunch is a bowl of ramen noodles, and dinner, perhaps, *tonkatsu* (deep-fried pork) served with shredded cabbage; no chance of eating from the thirty food groups here! At its best, however, many people still delight daily in the simple, traditional dishes of yesteryear, consuming substantial amounts of *wakame* (a dark green sea vegetable), tofu, and fermented soybeans.

Japan is not a country of vegetarians, despite a long tradition of vegetarian cooking in its Buddhist temples (called *shojin-ryori*), and the abundance of vegetable- and legume-based dishes that can be found in traditional Japanese cuisine. In fact, the idea of vegetarianism is almost foreign, illustrated by the fact that most modern Japanese opt to use the English term "vegetarian," should the need arise, rather than their own, perfectly good Japanese word, *sai-shoku-shugi-sha*. When one does admit to being a vegetarian, people generally express incredulity, and a barrage of questions begin. They often express the image they hold in their minds of vegetarianism being dark and bland, a meal centering around brown rice with a few vegetables, without color, excitement, or taste. Actually, many Japanese are uninterested in vegetarianism because they do not feel that it is necessary; they believe that their diet is already as healthful as possible. With their longevity statistics and the existence of more documented centenarians than any other nation, one would think that they are justified in this belief. Yet recent studies also reveal that stomach, intestinal, and breast cancer are all on the rise, as well as heart attacks and strokes. Japanese longevity so far may simply be due to the effects of what was once a healthful diet coupled with modern medicine; younger Japanese are not faring so well.

In contrast, I encountered many people (mostly women) who were sincerely interested in exploring the idea of approaching health through one's diet. In my many cooking classes and public cooking demonstrations at department stores in Japan, I found that most Japanese housewives were deeply intrigued by the idea of a vegetarian diet and its benefits. Although many admitted that making such a complete and drastic change would be difficult in their lives, they frequently promised to do their best to incorporate aspects of it into their diet (as they bowed and thanked me). Likewise, the past ten to fifteen years have seen the emergence of numerous natural food stores, which, though quite limited by American standards, have proven to be quite successful and popular, especially with female customers. Some young women even consider vegetarianism to be somewhat chic.

Animal rights, however, is a concept that is unheard of in Japan. This is a country with a tradition of whaling, where women consider it fashionable to flaunt furs, and the famous Kobe cattle are fed beer and massaged daily to produce the perfect marbleization of fat in the sweetest, most tender, most expensive beef—and diabetic cows. The best approach I found to introducing vegetarianism was to discuss its health benefits.

Trying to dine out in a strictly vegan fashion in Japan can present challenges. Although dairy products are not found in traditional Japanese cuisine, fish-based stocks appear in a range of dishes from appetizers to soups to entrées. This makes dining out difficult, although fine dining establishments may be willing to accommodate such a customer (albeit with surprise at the request). My advice to vegan or vegetarian visitors of Japan: find a temple or restaurant that serves traditional *kaiseki*-style *shojin-ryori* (Buddhist vegetarian cooking)—and splurge big time. You won't regret it.

The Recipes

It is important to understand that this is a vegan Japanese cookbook. Included are many recipes that are truly traditional—that is, recipes that are by definition vegetarian to begin with. In addition, I have also developed vegan recipes for dishes that traditionally would contain meat, fish, or fowl. These recipes do not exist in traditional Japanese cooking and, for the most part, do not even exist in shojin-ryori. In them, I have utilized nontraditional ingredients that produce traditional-tasting results, such as the *Chawan-Mushi* (Savory Custard Soup, page 64), an egg custard soup in which I have substituted silken tofu as the custard (most Japanese would be utterly amused by the idea), or the *Tonkatsu* (Deep-Fried Pork, Vegan-Style, page 153) that features seitan instead of pig.

Japanese dishes are usually flavored simply with just a few seasonings—soy sauce, mirin, miso, sake, sea salt, broth, and sugar. With the exception of Japanese chili pepper in a few select dishes, spices are generally not used. Where the saltiness of soy sauce is counterbalanced with sugar, I have substituted more healthful sweeteners such as brown rice syrup, FruitSource, or evaporated cane juice. Although not recommended for health reasons, sugar can be used if the alternative sweeteners are unavailable.

The Japanese Meal

The composition of the three basic meals served in Western cultures differs radically from traditional meals in Japan. In the U.S., sweet items are generally consumed at breakfast in the form of breakfast pastries, pancakes, waffles, cereals with sugar, or toast with jam. Lunches often consist of sandwiches, soups, salads, and other lighter fare, while dinners center on a meat entree or a heavier pasta or casserole dish. In Japan, the variances are not so great, and the same types of food are served at every meal, although meals earlier in the day tend to be simpler. Otherwise, there are virtually no dishes that are meant specifically for a certain time of of day and no other.

Rice, or *gohan*, is generally the centerpiece of every meal, unless some form of noodle is being served. *Gohan* also means "meal" and can refer to breakfast, lunch, or dinner. The other items are all meant to be eaten in small quantities as accompaniments to the rice. Gohan, in this sense "a meal," would not be complete without some soup, whether miso or *suimono* (clear soup). And generally, some *o-shinko* or *o-tsukemono* (pickles) would be served in small quantities. The other items, which would appear to the Westerner as either entrées or side dishes, are all lumped under a category called *okazu* (basically everything other than the trio of rice, soup, and pickles). This category would be divided based on methods of preparation, such as broiled foods, fried foods, boiled foods, those prepared with vinegar, and so on. In composing a meal, one would generally try to create a dish from each or several of these subdivisions. In this book, most of the chapters feature these subdivisions, and a perusal of them should arm you with several combinations.

For most family dinners, two to four okazu would be adequate, in addition to a soup, some optional pickles, and, of course, the rice. Although the rice served is usually short-grain white and unflavored, on certain occasions a flavored rice would be served. A perfect example of this would be in the fall when the luscious matsutake mushrooms come into season and one might make a special treat of *Matsutake Gohan* (Rice with Matsutake Mushrooms, page 44). Except for this sublime dish, I encourage you to serve brown rice as often as possible. (I have found that using a pressure cooker to cook brown rice yields the sticky texture that most resembles Japanese rice.)

Sometimes a single one-pot creation will suffice for an entire meal along with rice. These are called *nabe-mono* and are popular in cold weather when the family huddles around a gurgling ceramic pot filled with vegetables, tofu, and, typically, seafood. The most famous of these is *sukiyaki*, although many other forms with subtler flavors abound.

Meals featuring a noodle dish do not require rice and differ in composition. A popular simple lunch would be either soba or udon noodles, which fill a bowl brimming with tasty broth and perhaps some vegetables, seaweed, or fish. Generally, noodles comprise the whole meal, and okazu would not be served, except what is on top or alongside the noodles. In summer, cold noodles are served with dipping sauces and accompanied by the items that would be on top of them if they were served hot.

Dessert, when served, most often consists of seasonal fruit. In winter, a bowl brimming with *mikan* (Japanese mandarin oranges) would delight the family after most meals. In addition, a variety of colorful and beautifully shaped Japanese sweets made from ingredients such as *mochi* (pounded sweet rice), azuki bean paste, agar agar, soybean flour, and maple leaves may be served as an occasional special treat, usually with green tea in the afternoon. Another popular sweet is called *mitsumame*, a light dish featuring cubes of agar kanten (the Japanese equivalent of Jell-O), fruit, and azuki beans. Interestingly enough, one particular dish considered a refreshing dessert is not even sweet at all—*tokoroten*, a dish with noodle-like strands made from agar in a sauce of soy sauce, mirin, and Japanese hot mustard. In the same tradition, Japanese frequently eschew all sweets and opt for an *o-senbei* (a crisp, salty rice cracker) with green tea as the ending to a meal.

The evolution of dining and its impact on the meals served cannot be overlooked. One might say that the traditional Japanese breakfast—rice, miso soup, a little broiled fish, a few pieces of nori, and perhaps a raw egg to be mixed with soy sauce and poured over the rice—does not really go well with coffee. In a country such as Japan, where coffee houses abound and the art of brewing fine coffee has been elevated to an art form, connoisseurs will easily drop $5 for a cup of some master brew. (Many coffee houses feature unique ways of brewing coffee, and the better ones brew each cup to order.) And along with sipping coffee comes all the food that is associated with it, including bread, croissants, and pancakes. Thus, more frequently than not in increasingly busy urban areas, the traditional Japanese breakfast has been displaced by a continental breakfast.

Lunches have become Westernized as well, with Italian-style pastas infiltrating the soba market. Curry rice, pilafs, and *dorias* (rice topped with a cream sauce containing vegetables and seafood or meat) are highly popular, as are pizzas and sandwiches. Naturally, most of these items constitute single-item meals and are not, for the most part, balanced nutritionally.

Dinner is where the Japanese maintain a proclivity to dine in a traditional fashion. After all, they are Japanese, and the Japanese cannot go too many meals without rice and miso soup or they begin to miss them! Even here, however, some Japanese choose to forgo tradition and dine on Chinese, French, Italian, or the myriad other cuisines that are available throughout Japan.

Sample Menus

To eat Japanese-style, the following menus will guide you in assembling several dinners, either traditional or modern. *O-shinko* (Japanese pickles) are optional with each meal.

Fall or Year-round

steamed rice
Miso Soup with Daikon Radish and Fried Tofu Pouches
  (*Daikon to Abura-age no Miso Shiru*), page 57
Carrot and Tofu Scramble (*Iri-Dofu to Ninjin*), page 76
Spinach with Sesame Sauce (*Horenso no Goma-Ae*), page 97
Stewed Vegetables (*Ni-Mono*) page 125

Fall or Year-round

steamed rice
Wakame and Tofu Miso Soup (*Wakame to
  Tofu no Miso Shiru*), page 58
Fried Natto (*Natto-Age*), page 85
Cucumber Salad with Wa-Fu Dressing, page 105
Stewed Okara with Vegetables (*U-no-Hana*), page 133

Spring or Summer

Oyster Mushroom Pilaf (*Shimeji Gohan*), page 43
Clear Soup with Chrysanthemum Leaves
  (*Shungiku no O-Suimono*), page 65
Deep Fried Tofu in Broth (*Age-Dashi Dofu*), page 88
Daikon Salad with Lime-Ume Dressing
  (*Daikon Salada*), page 164
Spicy Braised Yam Cake (*Konnyaku no
  Itame-Mono*) page 127
Steamed Kabocha with Lemon Crème Fraîche
  (*Kabocha no Lemo Kureem Kake*), page 163

Year-Round

steamed rice
Tofu and Vegetable Stew (*Kenchin Jiru*), page 63
Tofu with Teriyaki Sauce (*Teriyaki Dofu*), page 78

Winter

steamed rice
Potato and Onion Miso Soup (*Jaga-Imo to Tamanegi no Miso Shiru*), page 59
Stewed Daikon with Sweet Miso Sauce (*Furofuki Daikon*), page 130
Tofu with An Sauce (*Tofu no An-Kake*), page 75
Stewed Kabocha Squash (*Kabocha no Ni-Mono*), page 128
Blanched Spinach or Greens (*Horenso no Hitashi*) 98
Braised Burdock Root (*Kimpira Gobo*), page 126

Year-Round

steamed rice
Deep-Fried Pork, Vegan-Style (*Tonkatsu*), page 153
shredded raw cabbage with *tonkatsu* sauce
miso soup of your choice

Year-Round

steamed rice
Sukiyaki, pages 122-123
Cucumber Salad with Wa-Fu Dressing, page 105

Fall

Rice with Matsutake Mushrooms
(*Matsutake Gohan*), pages 44-45
Miso Soup with Tofu and Scallions, page 61
Tempura, pages 90-94
Mushroom Salad (*Mushurumu to Shiso no Salada*), page 165

Summer

steamed rice
Dark Miso Soup with Nameko Mushrooms
(*Nameko-Jiru*), page 62
Cold Tofu (*Hiya-Yakko*), page 74
Fried Eggplant with Miso Sauce (*Nasu no Dengaku*), page 86
Roasted Asparagus with Lime Ponzu Sauce, page 168
Wakame Salad (*Wakame Salada*), page 101

Fall

Chestnut Rice (*Kuri-Gohan*), page 46
Savory Steamed Custard Soup (*Chawan-Mushi*), page 64
Tofu in Hot Water (*Yu-Dofu*), page 73
Tempura of Julienne Vegetables (*Kaki-Age*), page 94
Blanched Spinach or Greens (*Horenso no Hitashi*) 98
Mountain Yam with Plum Sauce (*Nagaimo no Ume Ae*), page
107
Enoki with Sake or White Wine (*Enoki-no-Saka-Mushi*), page 134

Year-Round
Savory Vegetable Pancakes (*Okonomiyaki*), page 145
fried noodles (*yaki-soba*)
green salad

Year-Round
Vegetarian Eel Over Rice (*Unaju or
    Unagi Donburi*), page 142
Japanese-Style Consommé (*Suimono*), page 66
Cucumber and Wakame Salad with Miso Dressing
    (*Kyuri to Wakame no Miso Dressingu Kake*), page 104

A Late Night "Snack"
Ramen
Japanese Potstickers (*Gyoza*), page 148

The following items constitute one-dish meals, accompanied by a small salad, soup, or a simple vegetable:

Curry Rice (*Karei Rice*), pages 146-147
Mushroom Doria, pages 157-158
Spaghetti with Mushrooms (*Kinoko Spaghetti*), page 162
Pasta with Shiso Pesto (*Supageti to Shiso no
    Basilico Sauce*), page 161
fried noodles (*yaki-udon*) with miso soup
Any type of rice dish with topping (*donburi*) with miso soup
Any type of hot or cold soba or udon noodles

A note on the Pronunciation of Japanese Terms

Japanese is phonetically simple, with a total of only fifty sounds. All vowels are pure and regular as in the following

A—ah as in art

E—eh, a short e sound as in red

I—a short i sound as in it

O—a shorter o sound than in open, like the o in Spanish pronunciation

The consonant G is always hard, as in get. Thus in age-mono, age has two syllables, a and ge.

Glossary
Ingredients, Kitchen Concepts, and Tools

Note: Some of the following terms will be followed by a parenthetical alternative preceded by an "O." The "O" is an honorific letter that precedes many Japanese words. Where this is given, the honorific version is the preferred term.

Abura-age (Fried tofu pouches)—*Abura-age* is made by deep-frying thin slices of tofu. The results of this culinary trick produce golden brown pouches that resemble a form of skin. Abura-age can be simmered in stock, soy sauce, and other flavorings to render a succulently flavored and textured soy product that can be added to noodles, vegetables, and other dishes. It can also be split open and stuffed with sushi rice to make *inari-zushi*. It is sold in plastic bags, usually in packs of three pouches.

Agar agar (kanten)—A tasteless, clear sea vegetable product that is the vegetarian equivalent of gelatin, made from a sea vegetable called *ten-gusa*. In the winter of 1647 Lord Shimazu of Kyushu discovered that a dish made from ten-gusa left outside in the cold froze overnight, then melted under the sun by day and then dried out. He called this freeze-dried product *kan-ten* (kan is the character for "cold," ten, for "heaven") and went on to invent its first dish, *tokoroten*, a dish of slippery kanten noodles.

Agar agar has virtually no calories and is high in fiber. It is available in three forms: bars, flakes, and powder. The bars must first be soaked in water for several minutes to soften, then they are squeezed and shredded by hand into the liquid used for dissolving them. The flakes can be added to the liquid, allowed to soften for a moment, then dissolved over heat. The powdered form is the easiest to use, requiring only whisking into the liquid. All forms of agar agar must be boiled for a couple of minutes to produce a gelling effect, although once gelled, they will remain congealed at room temperature. Dishes containing a high amount of an acidic ingredient, such as lemon juice, will require more agar agar to gel. The Japanese company Sokensha has a powdered form that is vastly superior to any other I have used. It renders a gelatinous quality that is very similar to gelatin. (Generally, agar agar produces a firmer, less "wobbly" texture than gelatin.)

Age-mono—Fried dishes.

Ajitsuke-nori—Nori that has been seasoned, usually with soy sauce, sugar, and MSG. It is pre-cut into little rectangles and packaged in little packets for individual use with rice. (With unseasoned nori, you would usually tear it yourself and dip in soy sauce to eat with rice.) If you choose to eat this kind of nori, try to find one without MSG.

An, Ankake—*An* is a lightly gelatinous sauce that is generally thickened by kuzu, arrowroot, or cornstarch. *Ankake* is a dish with an sauce poured over it.

Ao-nori—A flaked, bright green dried seaweed typically sprinkled on *yaki-soba* (fried noodles), *okonomiyaki* (Japanese savory pancakes), and other dishes.

Atsu-age—Deep-fried tofu blocks. Deep-frying forms a brown, tasty exterior and a firm interior. It is good for stir-fries, soups, sukiyaki, *nabe-mono* (Japanese hot pot), and simply with a little ginger, green onion, and soy sauce.

Azuki—Azuki beans are small red beans with a high sugar content. They are used to form a sweet bean paste for desserts and are simmered with sugar to make *zen-zai*, a sweet dessert soup with *o-mochi* (pounded rice cake).

Bento (O-bento)—A boxed lunch, usually consisting of a container of wood, metal, or plastic with several compartments, the largest for rice, and others for the various *okazu* (side dishes or entrées).

Cha (O-cha)—Green tea. This is the national drink, and it is consumed throughout the day.

Cha-wan (O-cha-wan)—Literally, "tea bowl." This can encompass a cup for tea or a bowl for rice (into which you might indeed pour tea; see *cha-zuke*, page 23).

Cha-wan-mushi (O-cha-wan-mushi)—A custard soup steamed in individual cups with lids. Usually made with *dashi* (stock) and eggs, it contains little "surprises" at the bottom, such as seafood, chicken, ginko nuts, shiitake mushrooms, and vegetables. It is considered a delicacy in Japan.

Cha-zuke (O-cha-zuke)—Rice with tea poured over it. It can be seasoned with other ingredients as well, including finely chopped vegetables or pickles, Japanese herbs such as shiso, or seafood.

Daikon (O-daikon)—A long, white, mild-flavored Japanese radish. Can be eaten raw or cooked.

Dango (O-dango)—Japanese sweet dumplings made of rice or sweet rice flour.

Dashi (O-dashi)—Japanese soup stock, traditionally made from konbu (a sea vegetable), *katsuobushi* (dried fish flakes), and sometimes dried shiitake. This becomes the basis for flavoring many dishes from soups and vegetables to entrées. Several recipes for vegetarian dashi are provided in this book.

Do-nabe—An earthenware pot, usually decorated on the outside, that can be placed directly over the heat. *Nabe-mono* (Japanese one pot meal) would be made in a large *do-nabe*. They can be purchased at Japanese hardware or supply stores and are relatively inexpensive.

Donburi (O-donburi)—A large bowl, particularly for individual use, either for noodles or the genre of rice dishes known by the same name. In these dishes, the rice is topped with savory meat, vegetables, eggs, or seafood. Juices or the sauce from the dish imbue the rice with flavor.

Enoki—A white mushroom with a long, thin stem and tiny cap, grown in little bundles. It has a very delicate flavor.

Fu—A light, puffy, bread-like product made from gluten. It is often colorful and made in various shapes. It is sold dried and reconstituted in soups, primarily *suimono* (consommé). Children love these!

Gen-mai—Brown rice. Although considerably more nutritious than white rice, brown rice is difficult to come by in Japan.

Gohan—Steamed Japanese rice; also means "meal" and can refer to any meal.

Goma—Sesame seeds. *Goma-shio* is a topping for sprinkling on rice. It is made from toasted, lightly ground natural or black sesame seeds and salt. Sesame seeds are high in calcium and can be used in a variety of ways to season foods.

Goma-abura—Toasted sesame oil. A few drops of this added at the end of cooking to stir-fries, soups, and sauces greatly enhances the flavor. Sesame oil has a low smoking point and is thus best used in combination with another oil, such as canola, for sautéing purposes. Some of the best tempura restaurants in Japan add sesame oil to their frying oil to impart flavor.

Goma-dofu—A silky, rich, slightly gelatinous "tofu" made from sesame butter.

Hakusai—Napa cabbage. Can be eaten cooked, raw, or pickled.

Hashi (O-hashi)—Chopsticks. Japanese chopsticks are shorter than Chinese ones. They are often lacquered and highly decorated.

Hijiki—A black, short, thread-like sea vegetable. High in calcium and iron, it is extremely flavorful.

Inari-zushi—See o-inori-san, page 28.

Kanten—See agar agar, page 21. A gelatin-like dessert made with agar agar that is firmer and less "wobbly" than Jell-O. Generally sold in dry form, it requires reconstituting in water before using.

Karashi—Bright yellow Japanese hot mustard. It usually comes in a powdered form that can be easily mixed with a little water and can also be found in a prepared form in a tube. It differs in flavor from most Western mustards and is hotter.

Katakuriko—Potato starch. Can be used like cornstarch.

Ko-me (O-ko-me)—Uncooked rice. Cooked rice is referred to as *gohan.*

Konbu—A stiff, green sea vegetable used primarily for flavoring *dashi* (stock). It is also used in thin strips to tie or bundle vegetables or other savory items.

Konnyaku—A white or grayish, opaque product made from the *konnyaku-imo* (mountain yam), konnyaku is unlike anything in Western cuisine and thus very hard to describe. It is sold in rectangular blocks packaged in plastic in the refrigerated section of Japanese food stores. Although it has little flavor, the slightly rubbery texture of konnyaku is interesting, and it can absorb other flavors and become quite succulent. It has virtually no calories and is very high in fiber. Konnyaku can be sliced and stewed, sautéed, or broiled.

Kuzu, Kuzu-ko—A high-quality thickening agent made from the ground root of the kuzu plant. It comes in small, rock-like chunks that dissolve easily in liquids. Kuzu is more concentrated than cornstarch, so less can be used. Because it is not refined like cornstarch, it is considered more healthful; in fact, it is said to possess many medicinal qualities. Arrowroot, cornstarch, or *katakuriko* (potato starch) can be substituted.

Lotus root—See renkon, page 29

Matcha—Japanese powdered green tea used for tea ceremonies. It is made in a very different manner from other teas in that it is not steeped in hot water. Rather, the powdered tea is mixed with hot water in the bowl from which it will be drunk with a little wooden whisk. The resulting tea is thick, opaque, almost milky, and has the flavor of the tea leaves. This is the tea that is used in so-called "green tea ice cream."

Matsutake—Literally translated as "pine mushroom." An aromatic, woody-flavored mushroom that is among the world's most expensive—it can fetch a cool $50 per pound. Fortunately, only a few are needed to flavor a whole pot of rice or soup. These are in season for only a brief time in the fall, and any dish with matsutake mushrooms is considered a delicacy.

Mirin—Japanese sweet sake. Used primarily for cooking (not drinking), it tempers the soy sauce or salt in a dish.

Miso (O-miso)—Fermented soybean paste. Miso is the basis for *miso-shiru* (miso soup), a staple in the Japanese diet. It is also an important flavoring agent in many sauces and dishes. A good light miso and a dark red one are musts in the Japanese cupboard. There are so many varieties of miso that a shopper can become utterly baffled as to which type to buy. Although miso is primarily made from soybeans, it can also contain rice, barley, or other grains, often with vastly different results. Miso that contains rice is often mellow and mild.

In general, the non-Japanese shopper need be concerned only about whether their miso is white or red. White miso tends to be milder and sweeter, while red is intense and salty. White miso is not pure white, however, and can range in color from straw to a light brown. It can be very smooth looking or somewhat lumpy. Red miso is really more of a dark brick brown.

Since there is such a great variation in flavor, it would behoove the shopper to inquire with the Japanese shopkeeper as to which misos they consider the tastiest. Many families in Japan have a particular brand of miso they prefer. Some brands may contain MSG, so it is wise to read the label. Also, due to recent concerns about diet and health and the sodium content of foods, reduced-sodium misos are available.

Mitsuba (Trefoil)—A delicately fragrant herb with a long stem. If you are lucky enough to find it, make yourself some *suimono* (clear soup) and top it with some of this wonderful herb. Its delicate and unmistakable flavor will permeate your mouth.

Mochi (O-mochi)—Pounded rice cake. *O-mochi* is traditionally made in a ritualistic, ceremonial fashion with men taking turns pounding hot, glutinous rice with a large wooden mallet. It almost verges on a dance. Within minutes, the rice begins to look like bread dough as it becomes stretchy and smooth. It can then be eaten fresh, rolled in a little *kinako* (soy flour), or broiled with nori and soy sauce. Nothing compares to fresh o-mochi, although the dried form is more readily available. Fresh o-mochi is shaped into small round cakes or flattened out, allowed to dry and harden, then cut into small rectangles. This is the traditional food of *O-sho-gatsu* (New Year's Day), when it makes an appearance in *O-zoni* (New Year's Soup) and other dishes.

Several natural food manufacturers in the U.S. now make o-mochi and sell it vacuum-packed either refrigerated or frozen. Japanese o-mochi is usually made from white rice, although *genmai-mochi* (brown rice mochi) can be found in natural food stores. American mochi can come in different flavors, including cinnamon raisin, although such flavorings are unheard of in Japan and could be considered heretical.

Myoga—Young ginger buds. These can be sliced and eaten raw, added to soups, or used as a garnish.

Nameko—A small, brown mushroom with a slightly slimy surface, usually sold in little packages or canned. Very good in dark miso soup.

Natto—Fermented soybeans. Sticky and slimy, natto is thought by some to have an offensive flavor, although many Japanese find it delicious. In fact, young children usually love it if they are exposed to it at an early age. Usually, it is simply mixed with soy sauce and *karashi* (hot Japanese mustard) and eaten over rice, although there are many other methods of preparation for this highly healthful food. Natto contains many digestive enzymes.

Nori—Sheets of dark (usually black) dried seaweed. Toasted, torn into little rectangles, and dipped in soy sauce, it is the perfect accompaniment to hot rice when you may not have many other items to eat. Children love to munch on plain nori as a snack. It can also be used in vegetarian dishes to lend a "fishy" flavor.

O-inori-san (Inari-zushi)—Literally meaning a "prayer" because, according to folklore, demonic foxes were said to like them, *o–inori–san* are rice balls stuffed in *abura-age* (fried tofu) pouches that have been simmered in a slightly sweet mixture of dashi (stock), soy sauce, and mirin.

Okara—Okara is the high-fiber by-product of tofu manufacturing. It is white, moist, and resembles clumped snow. It is usually stewed with vegetables and seasonings as a side dish.

Okazu—Because there are no entrées in a traditional Japanese meal, all of the dishes that accompany *gohan* (rice) are called *okazu*, whether they are as substantial as entrées or light as side dishes.

O-mi-o-tsuke—"Honorable miso soup," another term for the soup that completes any meal.

O-nigiri—Japanese rice balls seasoned with sea salt, containing a morsel of something good in the middle (typically *umeboshi* [salty pickled plums] or fish), and wrapped in nori or sprinkled with sesame seeds. The first item on the menu for any respectable Japanese picnic would be a selection of o-nigiri.

Oroshi-ki—A Japanese grater that reduces hard vegetables, such as daikon or ginger, to a pulp. It is flat with a little receptacle at the bottom where the grated substance can set during grating. It is inexpensive and extremely useful for grating ginger, as well as making *daikon-oroshi* (grated daikon) for tempura and other dishes.

Panko—Light, crispy, dried breadcrumbs. Coating food to be deep-fried in commercially available panko will produce vastly superior results than using homemade breadcrumbs. Although the ingredients may not be as "pure" as crumbs made from whole grain bread purchased from your local natural food store, sometimes the culinary results are worth sacrificing a little nutritional value.

Ponzu—A light dipping sauce made from a citrus juice, soy sauce, and mirin.

Ramen—The Japanese version of Chinese noodles in soup. In the U.S. it is known primarily in its dried, "instant" style and is sold in little cellophane packages with a small packet of powdered broth. If fresh ramen noodles are available (and contain no eggs), a stint in the kitchen producing steaming hot bowls of real ramen would prove quite worth the simple effort.

Renkon—Lotus root. Must be peeled before use. If not used immediately, immerse in water to prevent discoloration resulting from oxidation.

Rice vinegar (Su, O-su)—A very mild vinegar used to make dressings, pickles, and sauces. Available plain and seasoned with sea salt and a small amount of sugar.

Sake (O-sake)—Wine made from rice. Although the impression that many people have of sake is that it is always drunk hot, sake can be enjoyed either warm or cold. The best sakes, made by microwineries in Japan, are in fact most often enjoyed chilled. There are many varieties with different degrees of sweetness or dryness, as well as flavor. For cooking purposes, there is no need to buy an expensive bottle of sake; Japanese grocery stores carry magnums of perfectly adequate sake for $5 to $6.

Sansho—A slightly spicy Japanese herb, usually found in powdered form and sprinkled on *unagi* (eel).

Sashimi (O-sashimi)—Raw fish served with soy sauce and wasabi. The only vegetarian equivalent would be a high-quality konnyaku (page 25), thinly sliced. Some supermarkets in Japan feature delicately textured white or green konnyaku meant to be served sliced with *wasabi-joyu* (wasabi and soy sauce) in the style of sashimi.

Senbei (O-senbei)—Japanese rice crackers made from glutinous rice. The varieties are endless for this most delicious treat, an excellent snack with green tea. A classic example would be *nori senbei*, a rice cracker glazed in soy sauce and wrapped in nori. They are crunchy, tasty, and usually close to fat-free.

Sesame Oil—See goma-abura, page 24. In choosing sesame oil, always buy the dark toasted variety, not the clear oil made from raw sesame seeds.

Shamoji—A small wooden paddle-like utensil used for serving rice. Before using, a shamoji is dipped in water so that the rice will not stick to it. It is also used for "fluffing up" the rice before serving.

Shichimi-togarashi—A mixture of seven Japanese spicy peppers. It can be sprinkled in dishes to add heat and is often served with soba or udon noodles.

Shiitake—Black mushrooms. Available either fresh or dried. In purchasing shiitake, either fresh or dried, look for mushrooms that have the thickest looking caps. The highest quality, called *donko shiitake*, are far meatier, more flavorful, and silkier in texture than their thinner cousins. Dried donko shiitake will have caps that have deep cracks in them. To reconstitute dried shiitake, soak in cold or tepid water for several hours or overnight. Reconstituting in hot water expedites the process but sacrifices some of the flavor. The water used for soaking forms the base for delicious soups, dashi (stock), and sauces. Leftover reconstituted shiitake and the soaking liquid can be kept refrigerated for about a week.

Shinko (O-shinko)—Japanese pickles made from various vegetables. Served with most meals as an aid to digestion.

Shirataki—White or grayish noodles made from *konnyaku* (page 25). Like konnyaku, shirataki contains no calories and is a boon for dieters. Shirataki absorbs the flavors of the sauce or broth that it is simmered in, and is thus used for *sukiyaki*.

Shiso (O-shiso)—Perilla leaves or beefsteak plant leaves. A cousin of our basil, *shiso* is a highly decorative and fragrant herb with a hint of mint. Equally befitting Japanese and Western dishes, the beautiful large leaves can be ground into a shiso pesto sauce or rolled up with avocado and natto to make a delicious sushi. There are numerous recipes here with shiso. Although I lack a green thumb and have not been successful growing much of anything, my mother has found that shiso is very easy to grow. This is a good idea for someone living in an area where it is not available since it is such a delightful and versatile herb.

Shoyu (O-shoyu)—Japanese soy sauce. Japanese soy sauce is traditionally made from soy beans, wheat, and sea salt through a natural fermentation process. Shoyu is the essential seasoning in Japanese cuisine; trying to cook Japanese food without soy sauce would be tantamount to cooking authentic French food without butter. The most widely available, high-quality soy sauce in the U.S. is Kikkoman. In Japan, many varieties exist with a wide range of prices, although most households use Kikkoman or equivalent brands. The Japanese soy sauce most commonly found here is referred to as *koi-kuchi shoyu*, or "dark-taste soy sauce."

Although it can be universally used for any dish in this book, its cousin, *usu-kuchi shoyu* (light-taste soy sauce, which is paler in color though saltier in taste), is preferable for *suimono* (clear soup) where a dark color is not desirable.

For those with wheat allergies, *tamari-joyu* (tamari) is available in most natural food stores. Tamari is made only from soybeans and has a darker, richer flavor.

Soba (O-soba)—Japanese noodles made with a high percentage of buckwheat flour. Most soba noodles contain wheat as well, since buckwheat lacks the gluten to produce the elasticity desired. Soba made from 100 percent buckwheat flour is called *ju-wari soba*; 80% buckwheat noodles are called *hachi-wari soba*. Unless this is written on the package, assume most soba on the market is made with far less buckwheat flour. Soba can be served hot in broth or cold, dipped in sauce. Although fresh soba noodles are sometimes available, they are most readily available dried.

Somen—Japanese vermicelli, white, often with a few colored strands (such as pink) thrown in for aesthetics. Generally slurped up icy cold during the hot summer months.

Sosu (O-sosu or Tonkatsu sosu)—This borrowed term for sauce has taken on new meaning in Japan. "Sauce," a thick, brown concoction with a flavor resembling Worcestershire sauce, is as ubiquitous in Japan as soy sauce. It is served over *tonkatsu* (deep-fried pork), *kushi-age* (fried skewered foods), and other items that have typically been coated in bread crumbs and deep-fried, as well as *okonomiyaki* (Japanese savory pancakes) and *yaki-soba* (fried noodles). No Japanese kitchen would be complete without it. Available in many brands and, principally, three different viscosities (thin, regular, and thick—their use depending on the flavors desired or type of dish being prepared).

Soy sauce—See shoyu, page 31.

Su (O-su)—Vinegar, typically rice vinegar. Rice vinegar has a low acidity and is thus very mild. Dressings made with rice vinegar require less oil to balance the acidity.

Suimono (O-suimono)—Literally "water dish," this is the Japanese equivalent of consommé. Often served in place of miso soup.

Su-no-mono—Literally translates as "vinegared dish." It includes raw vegetables, sea vegetables, and seafood tossed with a vinegar-based dressing and served as an appetizer or side dish.

Suribachi—A Japanese ceramic mortar and wooden pestle. The mortar has grooves which facilitate grinding and smashing seeds and nuts.

Sushi (O-sushi)—Probably the most popular Japanese dish in America! Sweet, vinegared rice formed into small cakes and topped with various types of raw fish, vegetables, or eggs. Vegetarian sushi featuring cucumber, shiitake, avocado, and other vegetables are also popular (see pages 48-51).

Takenoko—Bamboo shoots. Available fresh or canned, although fresh is far superior.

Takuan—Pickled daikon radish, often colored with yellow food coloring. Natural takuan is hard to find, although it is generally superior in flavor.

Teriyaki—A marinade or sauce made from soy sauce, sugar or other sweetener, and mirin. Many types of food can be made teriyaki-style.

Tofu (O-tofu)—Perhaps the most misunderstood food in America, tofu has had a long and reputable history in Japan. It has long been touted as a health food, promoting longevity and aiding in weight loss. Recent studies here have shown tofu to be rich in phytoestrogens that help prevent breast and ovarian cancer. Made in a similar manner to cheese, tofu is the product of pressing the curds that have separated from the whey in coagulated soymilk. Americans might call it bland; the Japanese prefer to think of it as delicate in flavor. Although different consistencies of tofu can be found in the United States ranging from soft to very firm, Japanese tofu is generally what might be labeled "regular" or firm. There are two types of tofu in Japan: momen (cotton) and kinugoshi (silk-strained; silken). They are made in a slightly different manner with different results, the former being the more common "regular" tofu that is usually found fresh in American markets, and the latter, the ultra-smooth, silky type that often comes in aseptic boxes (widely distributed by Mori-Nu). Silken tofu, unlike regular tofu, is not pressed. Unless silken tofu has been specified in a recipe, use regular tofu. Always choose fresh tofu; if it has a sharp smell, it will probably taste sour.

Tonkatsu sauce—See sosu, page 32.

Tororo-konbu—Sea vegetable shavings with a slightly acidic, salty flavor. Can be served as an instant soup by adding hot water and a dash of soy sauce.

Tsukemono (O-Tsukemono)—Japanese pickled vegetables. See *Shinko (O-shinko)*.

Tsuyu (O-tsuyu)—A soup or broth for noodles or a thin sauce for dipping noodles or other items. *Ten-tsuyu* is a dipping sauce for tempura.

Udon—Fat, white flour noodles made from wheat.

Umeboshi—Salty pickled plums made from a particular variety of Japanese plums (not the sweet variety that typically grows here). Said to kill stomach viruses and aid in digestion, it is often given during illness along with o-kayu (rice gruel). During World War II, an o-bento (lunch box) with rice and a single umeboshi plum in the center represented the Japanese flag and was often all some citizens ate. Try to find some without red food coloring. They are generally paler in color.

Wakame—A dark green, common sea vegetable often served in miso soup or salads. It can be purchased dried or fresh-packed in sea salt. If purchasing dried wakame, look or ask for "cut wakame" or "salad wakame," which is more tender than the type in long strands. The "cut" or "salad" variety reconstitutes much faster and can be thrown as is into your miso soup, while the type in long strands must first be soaked, cut, and then sometimes simmered if it is especially tough. The cut variety expands about 8 to 10 fold, so watch the portions! If fresh wakame is used, be sure to rinse out the sea salt, then soak and rinse again.

Wasabi—A green Japanese horseradish with a pungent flavor. A big dab will overwhelm all but the staunchest horseradish aficionados! Wasabi is a natural accompaniment to sushi and soy sauce. It is usually sold in a powdered form that is mixed with a small amount of water to form a paste, but can also be found in tubes. Fresh wasabi, however, is incomparable in flavor and fragrance, although it is virtually impossible to come by in the United States. *Wasabi-joyu* is soy sauce with wasabi.

Yaki-do—Grilled tofu. Sold in plastic packages, it is a firm-textured tofu with distinct grill marks on it.

Yama-imo—Mountain yam. Long, tan, hairy tubers that are peeled, then grated or sliced.

Yuba—A soy product made by removing and drying the skin that forms on soymilk when it is heated. Usually sold in a dried form in plastic packages, it is very fragile. It must be reconstituted to form a soft consistency before being used. If available, Chinese yuba is often sold in frozen form and is sturdier.

Yuzu—An aromatic Japanese citrus fruit, used primarily for its fragrant rind. Lemons or limes can be substituted but will give different results.

Rice Dishes

Gohan

G*ohan*, the Japanese word for rice, is also the word for meal. It signifies the importance of this highly revered grain to the Japanese people. The rice eaten by Japanese today is white short grain and slightly sticky, with the best varieties having a sheen to them. It forms the foundation of almost every meal, and most traditional Japanese dishes are designed to be consumed with it. Most Japanese who go too long without Japanese rice (while travelling, for example) grow lonely for it.

Until the Edo period (late 19th century), only the nobility consumed polished white rice. Due to the lack of B vitamins in white rice, noblemen began to fall ill with beri beri. Still, the general populace adopted similar eating habits, and today it is extremely difficult to procure brown rice in Japan. I lived next to a neighborhood rice store where rice was polished and sold everyday, and yet I could not convince the owner to sell me brown rice. In fact, he was incredulous the first time I asked. Many people of my mother's generation shudder when they recall having to endure the dreariness of brown rice during wartime.

Today, there is a small but growing movement towards more sustainable agriculture and a natural diet in Japan. Cooperatives are springing up everywhere, making the availability of the natural grain greater than ever before.

In a country where rice is the staple at almost every meal, one would think that it would be cheap. Unfortunately, quite to the contrary, rice can go for two or more dollars per pound by today's exchange rates. Because it is the national grain, rice production is largely protected by the government, and rice farmers (practically heroes) are handsomely subsidized. Although many Japanese favor the importation of cheaper rice from California and other parts of the world, at present there still remains an embargo on importing rice.

From a culinary perspective, every Japanese woman used to learn how to cook rice to perfection. In sushi restaurants, an apprentice in olden days would have to spend up to two years just cooking rice until it was perfect. Now, electric rice cookers have taken the mystery out of the method as long as one can measure accurately. Japanese rice is delicious eaten plain hot, cold, or formed into *onigiri* (rice balls wrapped in nori and enclosing a secret filling). It is also cooked with various mushrooms, vegetables, and seasonings for special occasions or turned into delicious and simple brothy concoctions that could be considered Japanese risottos. Of course, sushi rice, seasoned with vinegar and a little sugar and sea salt, is the foundation for a simple but grand style of cuisine. Although traditionally all of these rice dishes begin with white rice, it is possible to substitute more nutritious short-grain brown rice; in fact, once you become accustomed to the flavor of brown rice, you may find white rice to be somewhat bland!

Cooked Rice

Gohan

Yes, you can cook rice without a rice cooker, even though this fact might be seriously questioned by many young Japanese housewives. A heavy bottomed pot with a tight fitting lid is all that is necessary for most rice; for brown rice, I find that a pressure cooker yields a moister, stickier rice with a better texture than that cooked in a covered saucepan.

The method for cooking either white or brown rice is the same; only the length of time and proportion of rice to water change. Both types of rice benefit from being washed and soaked at least 30 minutes, or even several hours, before being cooked. The rice will cook slightly faster and be more tender. You can wash rice before going to work, leave it soaking in the water it will cook in, and then cook it upon returning in the evening. When washing white rice, fill the pot with cold water, stir the rice vigorously with your hand (the water will turn milky and cloudy), and then pour off the water. Repeat this until the water runs fairly clear. Pour in about 20% more water than white rice (about a knuckle above the rice). Allow this to soak for at least thirty minutes. (The longer the rice soaks, the more tender it will be.) Brown rice will not turn the water milky, but should be rinsed several times anyway. As a general rule, water should come up about two knuckles above the brown rice; for those who like to measure, for every 2 cups of brown rice, use 3½ cups of water. Less water is required if using a pressure cooker.

After washing and soaking, put a lid on the pot and turn the heat to high. When the water comes to a rolling boil (you will be able to hear it— no need to remove the lid), turn the heat to medium and cook for 5 minutes for white rice, 20 for brown. Then turn the heat as low as possible, and cook for another 5 to 10 minutes for white, 20 to 25 for brown. Do not remove the lid while cooking, and do not stir. Turn the heat off and allow to sit for 5 to 10 minutes before serving. Before serving, use a *shamoji* (a wide, flat spatula for rice, usually made of wood) or a wooden spoon to stir and fluff the rice.

A pressure cooker will cook brown rice in about 15 to 20 minutes after reaching 15 pounds pressure. Check the instructions for your particular cooker. Pressure cooking brown rice will yield a less dry, more desirable texture.

Zosui is the Japanese version of risotto, a brothy concoction of rice and tasty tidbits of vegetables, mushrooms, and seasonings. Although homey and simple, it is quite satisfying and a great way to use leftover rice from the day before.

Yield: 4 to 6 servings

Mushroom and Carrot Zosui

Mashurumu to Ninjin no Zosui

4 to 5 cups *Konbu to Shiitake no Dashi* (Konbu-Shiitake Stock), page 54, or 2 x 3-inch piece konbu, 8 to 10 dry shiitake, and 4 to 5 cups water

8 ounces *shimeji* (oyster mushrooms)

2 medium carrots, split in half and cut in half-moons

3 cups white or brown cooked rice

1 teaspoon sea salt

3 tablespoons soy sauce

⅓ cup thinly sliced scallions or green onions

If you do not have any shiitake-konbu stock on hand, soak the konbu and shiitake in the 4 to 5 cups water for 10 minutes in a saucepan, then partially cover and cook for 15 to 20 minutes, or until the shiitake is completely tender. Remove the shiitake and either reserve for another dish, or slice and return to the stock. If you already have the stock available, simply heat. Add the mushrooms and simmer for 2 to 3 minutes. Add the carrots, rice, and sea salt; cover and simmer for 10 to 15 minutes, stirring occasionally. Add the soy sauce, simmer for another 3 to 4 minutes, and adjust the sea salt to taste. Pour into individual bowls and top with the sliced scallions. Serve immediately.

Mixed Vegetable Zosui

Yasai Zosui

3 cups cooked rice

4 to 5 cups *Konbu Dashi* (Konbu or Konbu-Shiitake Stock), page 54

2 tablespoons sake

1 teaspoon sea salt

2 to 3 cups vegetables of choice, sliced, juliened, or finely diced (Good vegetables to use are broccoli, asparagus, green beans, snap peas, snow peas, sweet potatoes, squash, lotus root, leeks, carrots, mushrooms, etc. Do not use tomatoes, avocados, lettuce, cabbage, cucumbers, or beets.)

3 tablespoons soy sauce

¼ cup thinly sliced green onions

This is a flexible dish that allows you to use up whatever leftover veggies may be in the refrigerator. Alternatively, this can be a feast with carefully planned vegetable combinations fresh from the garden.

Combine the rice, stock, sake, sea salt, and root or hard vegetables (carrots, lotus root, etc.) in a pot, and bring to a simmer. Simmer for 15 to 20 minutes, adding the other vegetables in order of hardness, adding delicate snow peas or asparagus only towards the end. Stir occasionally. Add the soy sauce and simmer for another 3 to 4 minutes. Stir in the thinly sliced green onions, remove from the heat, and serve.

Yield: 4 to 6 servings

Rice is often cooked along with other ingredients such as vegetables, chestnuts, or mushrooms to create a fat-free dish similar to pilaf. Here is a simple version utilizing vegetables available year-round. Feel free to substitute other seasonal vegetables as desired.

Yield: 8 servings

Japanese Pilaf

Maze Gohan

3 cups short-grain brown or white rice

5 cups *Konbu Dashi* (Konbu or Konbu-Shiitake Stock), page 54 for brown rice, or 3½ cups for white rice

2 tablespoons sake

¼ cup soy sauce

8 ounces mushrooms, sliced

2 carrots, cut into 1-inch matchsticks

1⅓ cups frozen green peas

In a large pot or rice cooker, combine the rice and stock. Add the sake and soy sauce. Place the vegetables on top. Cover with a lid, and either turn on the rice cooker or bring the rice to a boil over high heat. Immediately turn the heat down, and continue to cook for 45 to 50 minutes for brown rice, or 10 to 15 minutes for white rice. Turn off the heat and allow to set for an additional 10 to 15 minutes. With a shamoji (flat, wide wooden rice spatula) or a wooden spoon, fluff the rice up and serve immediately.

Oyster Mushroom Pilaf

Shimeji Gohan

3 cups short-grain brown or white rice

4½ cups *Konbu Dashi* (Konbu or Konbu-Shiitake Stock), page 54 for brown rice, or 3¼ cups for white rice

¼ cup sake

3 tablespoons soy sauce

1 teaspoon sea salt

8 ounces *shimeji* (oyster mushrooms), rinsed and torn into small pieces

Wash the brown rice thoroughly. Combine with the other ingredients in a heavy pot with a tight fitting lid. Turn the heat to high, and bring to a boil. Immediately turn the heat down as low as possible, and cook for approximately 45 minutes for brown rice, or 10 to 15 minutes for white rice. Turn the heat off and allow to set for at least 10 minutes before serving. With a *shamoji* (flat, wide wooden rice spatula) or a wooden spoon, fluff the rice up and serve immediately.

Japanese oyster mushrooms lend a woodsy flavor to this rice.

Yield: 6 servings

Here is an autumnal specialty featuring one of the most expensive mushrooms in the world—the matsutake. This savory mushroom with a woodsy flavor is most aromatic and just a few of them will flavor an entire pot of rice.

Yield: 4 to 6 servings

Rice with Matsutake Mushrooms

Matsutake Gohan

3 cups short-grain white rice

2 pieces *abura-age* (fired tofu pouches), page 21

Approximately 5 ounces matsutake mushrooms

2 tablespoons soy sauce

1 tablespoon usu-kuchi shoyu, if available
(otherwise, increase soy sauce by 1 tablespoon)

2 tablespoons sake

Additional water for cooking rice

Wash the rice until the water runs clear, then place in a colander and allow to dry completely. Bring a pot of water to boil, place the pieces of abura-age in it, and boil for 30 seconds. Remove the abura-age and squeeze out the water and oil. Slice very thinly and set aside.

Clean the mushrooms by wiping gently with a damp towel. To preserve their flavor, do not rub and do not rinse under water. Slice them very thinly. Place in a bowl and pour the soy sauce, usu-kuchi shoyu, and sake over them. Allow to soak for 30 minutes. Wring the slices in your hands, squeezing as much of the mushroom liquid out as possible. Reserve the liquid.

Place the rice in a heavy-bottomed pot or electric rice cooker. Add the mushroom soaking liquid and enough additional water to make 3½ cups liquid.

To cook on the stove top, cover and bring to a boil, then turn down the heat to low and continue cooking for about 15 minutes; or follow the directions for your rice cooker. When finished, add the matsutake slices to the pot, cover, and let set for 15 minutes. With a *shamoji* (flat, wide wooden rice spatula) or wooden spoon, mix and fluff up the rice, and serve immediately.

Chestnuts are beloved by the Japanese and make an appearance in this unusual dish—a fall specialty.

Chestnut Rice

Kuri Gohan

12 ounces chestnuts

3 cups white or brown rice

3½ cups water for white rice, or 5 cups water for brown rice

1 teaspoon sea salt

2 tablespoons mirin

Spread the chestnuts on a cookie sheet, and roast in a 350°F oven for about 40 minutes. With a sharp knife, remove the chestnut shells, peeling off the brown skins if necessary. (They are very bitter.)

Wash the rice and add the water, sea salt, and mirin in a pot or rice cooker. Add the shelled chestnuts, cover, and cook 15 minutes for white rice or 45 to 50 minutes for brown rice. Let set for 10 to 15 minutes. With a *shamoji* (flat, wide wooden rice spatula) or wooden spoon, mix and fluff up the rice, and serve immediately.

Yield: 6 servings

Rice with Tea

Ocha-Zuke

Traditionally in Japan, one never puts anything on his rice—no soy sauce, butter, or gravy—with the exception of tea. Served with the proper condiments, ocha-zuke is delicious and a wonderful late night snack with leftover rice. There are many condiments possible, and today even instant ocha-zuke tea-condiment combos are available. (All you add is rice and hot water.) After trying these suggestions, you will not think that tea on rice is such a strange concept.

Per serving in a rice bowl:

Cooked rice, white or brown, preferably warm

Prepared green tea

One or more of the following condiments:

Very thin strips of nori

Finely chopped tsuke-mono (Japanese pickled vegetables—many varieties are available)

Slivered leaves of shiso

Slivered *myoga* (baby ginger shoots)

Toasted or blackened sesame seeds

Thin strips of cooked konbu from making stock

Wakame

Sansai (Japanese mountain vegetables, available in packets or frozen)

Place the condiments on top of the rice, and pour hot green tea to cover. If necessary, add a dash of sea salt.

I recall as a child coming to the United States and discovering that Americans put butter on their rice. I was appalled and sickened. I felt even more disgusted when a friend told me she enjoyed pouring sugar and milk on her rice. (Since then, of course, I have adapted well to Western cuisine and now enjoy hot rice cereal with vanilla soy milk!) But here is a simple way of eating rice beloved by Japanese that has made American jaws drop upon hearing it described—pouring green tea over rice.

Sushi is a practically a national pastime in Japan. Delicate fish served in the raw coupled with a slightly sweet, vinegared rice is almost a raison d'être for many Japanese. This is a dish that does not offer as many alternatives for the vegetarian, although some good ones do exist. This is also the one rice dish where I usually make a concession to white rice, although I have made and served brown rice sushi. (Somehow, it lacks the delicacy I associate with sushi.)

Yield: 6 to 12 servings
depending on appetites

Sushi Rice

Sushi Meshi

8 cups white rice

8 cups water

1 cup sugar, rice syrup, or FruitSource

1⅓ cups rice vinegar

2 tablespoons mirin

3½ tablespoons sea salt

Cook the rice in the water as instructed in the basic recipe on pages 38 and 39. It will be slightly firm. Combine the sweetener, vinegar, mirin, and sea salt in a pot, and bring to a boil. Turn off the heat and allow to cool.

Transfer the cooked rice to a large bowl or vat. With a large wooden spoon or *shamoji* (wide, flat wooden rice spatula), stir and fold the rice as you add the sushi vinegar a little at a time. The rice will absorb the liquid. If the rice stops absorbing the liquid, do not add any more. It should be moist but not wet or gummy. Traditionally, the rice is fanned to cool it and prevent it from becoming gummy as the vinegar is added; this is a great job for a youngster!

Sushi rice should not be refrigerated after being made, as it turns hard. If you are not serving it

soon, cover and leave at room temperature until serving time. Sushi rice can be made several hours in advance.

To make hand-rolled *nigiri-zushi* for your sushi party, you will need the following:

Toasted sheets of nori, cut in half

Wasabi (Japanese horseradish; available in powdered form as well as in prepared tubes)

Soy sauce

In addition, you will need some or all of the following for fillings:

Avocados, cut into strips (delicious!)

Cucumbers, cut into sticks (preferably Japanese; if using the English variety, peel and seed)

Thin slices of grilled or sautéed eggplant (not traditional, but good)

Carrot sticks, cooked in a little water with a dash or two of soy sauce and mirin or sweetener

Fresh shiitake, cooked in the *ni-mono* style (see page 125)

Burdock root, cut into matchsticks and cooked in the *ni-mono* style (see page 125)

Fresh shiso leaves—fragrant and wonderful!

Also, sugar is the standard sweetener for the sushi vinegar, since it is a sweetener with no inherent flavor. If using a liquid sweetener as a substitute, be sure to use one that is very mild in flavor, such as rice syrup, or FruitSource.

Here is a basic recipe for cooking sushi rice, followed by suggestions for serving "okonomi-zushi," or sushi-as-you-like-it, at home. It makes an ample amount of rice, since this is the meal and not a grain supplement to other dishes. Invite some friends and have a sushi party! (For a family meal, cut the portions in half)

Natto mixed with soy sauce and green onions

Kaiware (daikon sprouts—delicate but spicy)

Thin strips of smoked tofu (not traditional, but it works)

Blanched asparagus

Blanched spinach

Wakame, juliened and tossed in a little sesame oil and sea salt

Pickled ginger

To serve, line all the filler ingredients on a large platter or two. Provide small individual plates for each person to place his or her soy sauce and wasabi. Each person then takes a piece of nori, places a couple of tablespoons of rice on one end, applies wasabi lightly (if desired), then adds a filling of choice. The nori is then wrapped to form a cone (see illustrations). It is then dipped in the soy sauce and devoured with gusto! Serve icy cold Japanese beer and/or green tea along with it and have a vegan sushi feast.

Sushi Rice in Age Pouches

Inari-Zushi (or) O-Inori-San

3 cups white or brown rice

3 cups water for cooking white rice, or 4½ cups water for cooking brown rice

⅓ cup sugar, rice syrup, or FruitSource

1 tablespoon mirin

1 tablespoon sea salt

⅓ cup rice vinegar

6 to 12 *abura-age* (fried tofu pouches), page 21 (depending on size; they should be about 2 x 3-inches; if large, cut in half)

1 cup *Konbu Dashi* (Konbu Stock), page 54

2 tablespoons mirin

2 to 3 tablespoons soy sauce

3 tablespoons FruitSource, or sugar, or 5 tablespoons rice syrup

Cook the rice in the water according to the basic instructions on pages 38 and 39. Follow the sushi rice recipe on page 48 for making sushi vinegar with the 1 tablespoon mirin, the sea salt, and vinegar, and adding it to the rice.

To make the seasoned *abura-age* (fried tofu pouches), place the age pouches along with the konbu stock, 2 tablespoons mirin, soy sauce, and sweetener in a pot with a tight fitting lid. Bring to a simmer and cook for 10 to 15 minutes, or until the age pouches have absorbed the flavor. Let cool before handling. Remove the age pouches from the remaining liquid. Split open into pockets. Fill each pouch with sushi rice.

This was a favorite food of mine as a child—sweet sushi rice wrapped in a tasty age pouch; great finger food for picnics or lunch boxes.

Yield: 6 servings

Soups and Stews

Almost every Japanese meal is served with some type of soup. The most common is *miso-shiru*, or miso soup, a deceptively simple broth with a myriad possibilities for *gu* (the savory items that are cooked in the miso broth). Next to miso soup is *suimono*, literally water soup, a rather delicate and clear Japanese version of consommé. In addition, there are heartier stews and a famous custard soup made with eggs, for which I present vegan versions.

All of these soups and stews derive their delicate flavor from the broth used. Although broths from *bonito* shavings (tiny dried fish) are commonly used, full-flavored vegetarian broths are also made from *konbu*, a thick sea vegetable, and dried shiitake.

A visitor to Japan or a Japanese restaurant will find that soups, with the exception of *chawan-mushi* (egg-custard soup) are served without spoons. The small bowls are simply lifted to the lips and sipped without the aid of any utensils, except perhaps chopsticks to get at some of the *gu*.

Basic Miso Soup

O-Miso-Shiru (or) O-Mi-O-Tsuke

This most simple and basic soup can be absolutely gratifying and satisfying. Although it is extremely simple in its preparation, it has endless possibilities due to the various types of miso available and the ingredients that can be added. Vegetables, tofu, or sea vegetables are simmered briefly in the stock, and the miso is added at the end. The whole process can take anywhere from 5 to 15 minutes, depending on what type of *gu* or savory ingredients you use. The most important rule to remember for preparing the tastiest, and in fact the most healthful, miso soup is to add the miso last after the heat has been turned off. This preserves the delicate flavor of the miso, and also the friendly bacteria in the miso that are killed by high heat. It is almost impossible to give exact proportions for the amount of miso to stock, since miso varies greatly in saltiness and flavor. Dark miso is generally saltier and heavier in flavor than light miso. Misos made with rice or barley are sometimes sweeter. There are also some misos with a reduced salt content or even added broth; all of this will affect the amount to be added. Thus, it is always better to start off with the lesser amount and increase it as needed to taste. Generally speaking, ¼ to ½ cup of miso is added to a quart of konbu or shiitake konbu stock.

Variations for miso soup include sliced eggplant (simmer in *dashi* [stock] until tender), *Nameko-Jiru* (Dark Miso Soup with Nameko Mushrooms page 62), lotus root, even delicate asparagus. Please, no tomatoes, however—they are not a traditional ingredient and their flavor does not lend itself well to this use.

Here are three basic stocks that can be used in a variety of soups and stews. The Konbu-Shiitake Stock below is a slightly richer broth.

Konbu Stock

Konbu Dashi

3 x 4-inch piece konbu
1 quart water

Soak the konbu in the water for 30 minutes. Bring to a boil and simmer for 15 to 20 minutes. Turn off the heat and remove the konbu. (The konbu can be sliced and added to stir-fried veggies, etc.)

Konbu-Shiitake Stock

Konbu to Shiitake no Dashi

3 x 4-inch piece konbu
5 large or 10 small dried shiitake
1 quart water

Soak the shiitake and konbu in the water for at least 2 hours. Bring to a boil and simmer for 15 to 20 minutes. Remove the shiitake and konbu; they can be used for other dishes.

Yield: 1 quart

Shiitake Stock
Shiitake no Dashi

15 to 20 dried shiitake
1 quart water

Soak the shiitake in the water for several hours. The water will become a light to dark brown. There is no need to simmer; it can be used as is.

Shiitake stock with shiitake soaking in it can be kept in the refrigerator ready to use for up to two weeks.

Yield: 1 quart

The Japanese rarely prepare their own dashi anymore. Instead, like Westerners who cannot be bothered to make their own soup stock from scratch and prefer to reach for a bouillon cube, the Japanese buy powdered fish or konbu stock. Most of these are loaded with MSG and other additives. Here is a simple recipe for making a full-bodied semi-instant stock. This keeps for several months.

Yield: 2 cups

"Instant" Konbu Dashi

1¼ cups small konbu pieces

¾ cup tororo konbu (available in Japanese food stores)

3 tablespoons evaporated cane juice or sugar

1 to 2 tablespoons sea salt

Combine all the ingredients in a blender until they are as powdered as your blender will make them. Store in a jar with a tight fitting lid. Use 1 to 2 tablespoons per quart of water.

For *suimono* (clear soups) where elegance and presentation are important, I recommend placing a tablespoon or two in a stainless steel tea ball or muslin bag and simmering for 10 minutes in the water. Remove the tea ball or bag before using the stock. (The contents of the bag can be added to sautéed vegetables, rice, etc.) If, however, you do not mind tiny pieces of sea vegetables in your soup, simply add the mixture to water and simmer by itself or with other ingredients.

Miso Soup with Daikon Radish and Tofu Pouches

Daikon to Abura-age no Miso Shiru

This is a warming combination for cold weather.

1½ to 2 cups daikon, cut into 1-inch sticks

1 quart *Konbu Dashi* (Konbu or Konbu-Shiitake Stock), page 54

1 package *abura-age* (fried tofu pouches), page 21, usually 2 to 4 pieces, sliced ¼ inch thick

⅓ to ⅔ cup miso (a combination of light and dark misos is good for this particular soup)

3 to 4 green onions, chopped or thinly sliced

Simmer the daikon in the dashi (stock) until tender. Add the *abura-age* (fried tofu pouches) and simmer for another minute. Turn the heat off. In a small bowl, combine the miso with a little stock to make a paste. Add to the pot and mix or whisk well. Add the green onions and serve immediately.

Yield: 4 to 6 servings

Wakame (a mineral–rich, leafy green sea vegetable) and tofu make a light addition to miso broth. Wakame comes in either a dried or fresh form, the latter being sold in the refrigerated section of Japanese food stores. Either form requires soaking in water before it can be used.

The fresh type is often packed in a lot of sea salt, which must be thoroughly rinsed off before using. Keep in mind that the dry form expands more than ten-fold when soaked, so that only a small amount is needed.

Yield: 4 to 6 servings

Wakame and Tofu Miso Soup

Wakame to Tofu no Miso Shiru

1 quart *Konbu Dashi* (Konbu or Konbu-Shiitake Stock), page 54

Approximately 1 cup reconstituted wakame, roughly chopped

8 to 12 ounces regular or silken tofu, cut into ⅓ to ½-inch cubes

⅓ to ⅔ cup light miso

Bring the stock to a simmer. Add the wakame and tofu, and simmer for 2 to 3 minutes. Turn off the heat and make a paste of the miso and a little *dashi* (stock) in a separate bowl, then whisk or mix into the pot. Serve at once.

Alternate method:
For fresher tasting wakame with a less slimy texture, use a type of dried wakame that is frequently sold as "cut wakame." It is finely cut and reconstitutes almost immediately in hot liquid. It can be added to the hot *dashi* (stock) along with the miso. Allow it to steep with the heat off for another minute. I prefer this type of wakame miso soup, although the first method is more traditional.

Potato and Onion Miso Soup
Jaga-Imo to Tamanegi no Miso Shiru

1 to 2 medium potatoes, peeled and cut into sticks

1 large onion, cut in half and thinly sliced

1 quart *Konbu Dashi* (Konbu or Konbu-Shiitake Stock), page 54

⅓ to ⅔ cup medium or dark miso (light can also be used)

Another cold-weather soup, hearty and full-flavored.

Simmer the potatoes and onion slices in the stock until tender, about 15 minutes. Turn off the heat and make a paste of the miso and a small amount of stock; whisk into the pot. Serve immediately.

Yield: 4 to 6 servings

A lighter miso soup for spring or summer.

Miso Soup with Chard, Kale, or Bok Choy

3 cups roughly chopped chard, kale, or bok choy

1 quart *Konbu Dashi* (Konbu or Konbu-Shiitake Stock), page 54

⅓ to ⅔ cup light miso

Simmer the greens in the stock for several minutes until tender. Turn off the heat and mix in the miso. Serve immediately.

Yield: 4 to 6 servings

Miso Soup with Tofu and Scallions

¼ to ½ **pound silken tofu**

2 to 3 **scallions**

1 quart *Konbu Dashi* (Konbu or Konbu-Shiitake Stock), page 54

⅓ to ⅔ **cup light miso**

Cut the tofu carefully into little ½-inch cubes. Sliver the scallions as thinly as possible.

Heat the *dashi* (stock) until it comes to a simmer. Add the tofu and allow to heat for a minute. Turn off the heat. Dissolve the miso into it, adjusting the amount to taste. Add the scallions and serve immediately.

This is a basic miso soup that can accompany anything.

It's my children's favorite.

Yield: 4 to 6 servings

61

This miso soup made with a slightly slimy, albeit tasty, mushroom called nameko must be made with dark miso. Actually, the hot soup dissolves most of the sliminess of the mushroom, rendering a hearty, flavorful soup.

Dark Miso Soup with Nameko Mushrooms

Nameko-Jiru

3 cups *Konbu Dashi* (Konbu Stock), page 54
One 4-ounce can nameko mushrooms
¼ pound silken tofu, cut into ½-inch cubes
⅓ to ½ cup dark miso
2 to 3 scallions, minced

Heat the *dashi* (stock) to a simmer. Add the nameko mushrooms and silken tofu cubes, and heat for a minute. Turn off the heat and dissolve the miso in the soup, adjusting the quantity to taste. Add the scallions and serve immediately.

Yield: 3 to 4 servings

Tofu and Vegetable Stew

Kenchin Jiru

About 7 cups slivered, sliced, or diced vegetables: traditionally, taro root, carrots, daikon, potatoes, and something green, such as snow peas

2 tablespoons oil

1 pound tofu

6 cups *Konbu to Shiitake no Dashi* (Konbu-Shiitake Stock), page 54

½ teaspoon sea salt

4 to 6 tablespoons soy sauce

1 to 2 teaspoons grated fresh gingerroot

1 teaspoon dark sesame oil

Prepare the vegetables so that they are all roughly the same size and thickness (all root vegetables cut into matchsticks, or sliced, etc.) so that they will cook evenly.

Heat the oil in a large pot. Crumble the tofu by hand, and add to the oil, sautéing for a few minutes. Add the vegetables and sauté for a couple of minutes more. Add the stock and sea salt, and bring to a simmer. Partially cover and cook until the vegetables are tender. Flavor with the soy sauce, cook for another couple of minutes, then turn off the heat. Stir in the ginger and sesame oil, and serve.

There is a legend that says a young monk once dropped a block of tofu with which he was to prepare a dinner for the monastery. With his broken tofu, he concocted this delicious, country-style soup. Other vegetables such as green beans, parsnips, or squash can be used if Japanese vegetables are unavailable.

Yield: 6 servings

Traditionally made with eggs, this soup is considered a delicacy in Japan and is often served for special occasions. The delicate egg custard flavored with stock, soy sauce, and sake has hidden treasures at the bottom: morsels of wild mushrooms, gingko nuts, and often shrimp or other seafood. Here I present a vegan version using silken tofu to replicate the eggs.

Yield: 4 servings

Savory Steamed Custard Soup

Chawan-Mushi

1 pound silken tofu

1 cup *Konbu to Shiitake no Dashi* (Konbu-Shiitake Stock), page 54

2 tablespoons soy sauce (preferably usu-kuchi)

3 tablespoons sake, white wine, or dry sherry

4 large fresh shiitake mushrooms (reconstituted dry are also acceptable), cut in half or quartered

4 to 8 spears asparagus (depending on thickness), cut into ½-inch lengths

8 to 12 ginko nuts, shelled

2 green onions, minced or thinly sliced

Purée the tofu, stock, soy sauce, and sake in a blender or food processor until very smooth. Distribute the mushrooms, asparagus, and ginko nuts equally in the bottom of four *chawan-mushi* dishes or ceramic coffee mugs. Pour the tofu mixture on top to fill the cups three-quarters full. Cover each cup with aluminum foil, and place the cups in a large pot. Fill the pot with water half-way up the cups, cover the pot with a lid, and bring the water to a boil. Turn down the heat and simmer gently until the custard has risen and set. Top each cup with green onions and serve immediately.

Japanese-Style Consommé

Suimono

Basic Suimono:

3 to 4 dried shiitake mushrooms, or a 2 x 2-inch piece of konbu

3 to 4 cups dashi made from two tablespoons of "Instant" Konbu Dashi, page 56

½ teaspoon sea salt

1 tablespoon sake

2 to 3 teaspoons soy sauce (preferably usu-kuchi) (It is slightly saltier but has a lighter color and will not darken the dashi [stock].)

Suggestions for items to float in the dashi (stock) (use no more than 2 to 3):

½ carrot, thinly sliced, and if possible, trimmed to resemble flowers

2 fresh shiitake mushrooms, sliced paper thin

Enoki mushrooms, separated into very small clumps

Shimeji (oyster mushrooms)

A few leaves of baby spinach per bowl

A few sprigs of mitsuba (trefoil), page 27, if available (Do not use scallions if using mitsuba.)

Minced scallions

A grating of lemon or yuzu zest per bowl

Several pieces *fu* (wheat puffs) per bowl

Suimono, literally meaning "water dish," are by far the most delicate of Japanese soups. They are the equivalent of consommé and are delicious if made with a rich stock. Here, the dashi or stock is of paramount importance or the soup will be bland and lacking in character.

For a vegetarian version, I recommend using the "Instant" Konbu Dashi recipe on page 56, supplemented by either additional konbu or dried shiitake mushrooms to yield a flavorful base for the soup.

Yield: 4 servings

With a few pieces of decoratively pared veggies, tofu, and fu (colorful wheat "puffs") floating on the surface, these subtle soups are simplicity itself.

Soak the dried shiitake in the *dashi* (stock) until fully reconstituted. Squeeze out the shiitake and remove. If you are using konbu instead, add it to the dashi, bring it to a boil, and simmer for 10 minutes. Remove the konbu. It is now ready to be simmered briefly with a vegetable or mushroom slices and seasoned, or simply seasoned and poured into individual bowls with scallions, mitsuba, fu, or tender greens, such as baby spinach, that will wilt upon contact with the hot soup.

If you are using carrots, fresh shiitake slices, enoki, or shimeji mushrooms, add them to the dashi and simmer gently for a few minutes until tender. This will add a greater depth and complexity to the flavor. Add the sea salt, sake, and soy sauce, and simmer for an additional minute only. If you are not adding any of these vegetables, simply add the seasonings to the dashi and heat for a minute. Turn off the heat, taste, and adjust the seasonings. It should be flavorful but subtle. Pour into individual bowls and top with minced scallions, a grating of lemon zest, or if available, mitsuba sprigs. (They are extremely fragrant—my pick for suimono.)

Clear Soup with Chrysanthemum Leaves

Shungiku no O-suimono

3 to 4 cups *Konbu Dashi* (Konbu or Konbu-Shiitake Stock), page 54

⅓ bunch *shungiku* (young chrysanthemum leaves), cut into 1-inch lengths

2 fresh shiitake, sliced paper thin

2 teaspoons soy sauce (preferably usu-kuchi)

Sea salt or more soy sauce, to taste

Bring the stock to a simmer. Add the *shungiku* (young chrysanthemum leaves) and shiitake, and simmer gently for about five minutes, or until the leaves are tender. Turn off the heat, add the soy sauce, and stir; adjust the soy sauce or sea salt. Serve immediately.

This simply prepared but exotic-sounding soup features the tender, young leaves of chrysanthemums. They are sold in bunches in Japanese markets in the spring and early summer and are eaten as a vegetable. The highly fragrant leaves are unlike any other leafy green in flavor, possessing an almost "perfumey" flavor that may not appeal to some Westerners. I find that this very fragrance lends a unique flavor to suimono (clear soups). Do not attempt to eat the leaves of chrysanthemums from flower shops; they may be sprayed with unwanted pesticides.

Yield: 3 to 4 servings

New Year's Stew with O-Mochi

Ozoni

New Year's Day is the biggest holiday in Japan. The whole country shuts down; no businesses are open for at least the first three or four days of the New Year. This is the time to make your rounds to visit all of your relatives and friends, eating and sipping hot sake at every stop, huddling under the thick comforter of the *kotatsu*, a heated table with a thick blanket over it. Traditionally, housewives would spend the days before the New Year cooking various dishes of a cuisine called *o-sechi ryori*. Vegetables, beans, tiny fish, eggs, and other little dishes were cooked in plenty of sugar, soy sauce, and sake to preserve them for days. This would allow them to be free from the chores of the kitchen during the New Year's celebrations. (Of course, they would still be expected to entertain.) Although most housewives today forgo this tradition, or simply order these dishes from the many stores and catering services that provide them, the one dish they do cook fresh on New Year's Day and for the next few days is *o-zoni*, a stew that features the thick, chewy, stretchy rice cake called *o-mochi*.

O-mochi has become quite popular in the United States among natural food aficionados and is available year round, yet in Japan it is eaten primarily (if not solely) during the weeks of New Year's. O-zoni is the most famous dish featuring o-mochi, and throughout different regions of Japan, as well as in various households, there are numerous versions. In the Kanto region around Tokyo where I was raised, o-zoni is typically a savory soup containing vegetables and chicken. (I wasn't a vegan at age 6.) Later, when I married a man from Tottori, several hundred miles southwest of Tokyo, I was surprised to find that their o-zoni was sweet, a "stew" of azuki beans cooked with sugar and o-mochi, a dish we Tokyoites called *zenzai*. Apparently, he was equally shocked when he moved to Tokyo to attend college and found that our o-zoni was salty!

New Year's Stew with O-Mochi

Ozoni

10 to 12 dried shiitake

6- to 8-inch piece of konbu

8 cups water

¼ pound enoki mushrooms

¼ to ½ pound *shimeji* (oyster mushrooms)

1 tablespoon oil

2 carrots, thinly sliced

7 to 8 taro roots, peeled and quartered

⅓ cup sake

1 to 2 teaspoons sea salt

2 to 3 tablespoons soy sauce (preferably usu-kuchi)

½ teaspoon grated peel of yuzu or lemon

1 bunch spinach, rinsed well with stems trimmed

At least twelve 2 x 2-inch pieces mochi (preferably more)

3 to 4 scallions, minced

2 bunches *mitsuba* (trefoil), page 27, chopped (optional)

Soak the shiitake and konbu in the eight cups of water in a large pot for several hours. Bring slowly to a boil. Lower the heat and simmer for 15 minutes. Strain the shiitake mushrooms and

Here is a vegan version of this wonderful traditional dish. Use this as a guide and feel free to add or subtract vegetables as is convenient or desirable. Even now, I do not feel right starting off the New Year without several bowls of my favorite stew.

Yield: 6 servings

allow to cool momentarily, then trim the stems and slice the mushrooms. Reserve the stock for later.

Cut the bottoms off of the enoki mushrooms to separate them into individual mushrooms or clumps of 2 or 3. Trim the bottom of the *shime-ji* (oyster) mushrooms, and tear them apart with your hands into individual mushrooms.

In another pot, heat the oil. Add the mushrooms and sauté for a couple of minutes. Add the carrots, taro root, sliced shiitake, stock, sake, and sea salt. Partially cover and simmer gently for 15 to 20 minutes, or until the vegetables are tender. Add the soy sauce and yuzu or lemon. Adjust the seasonings.

In the meantime, blanch or steam the spinach until just wilted. Rinse in cold water to stop the cooking process. Squeeze and cut into 1-inch lengths.

Cook the mochi. Traditionally, this is done with a special broiler that is placed over your gas burner. Lacking one of these, you can easily do this in your broiler or oven at a high temperature. Preheat the oven to 450°F. Place the mochi

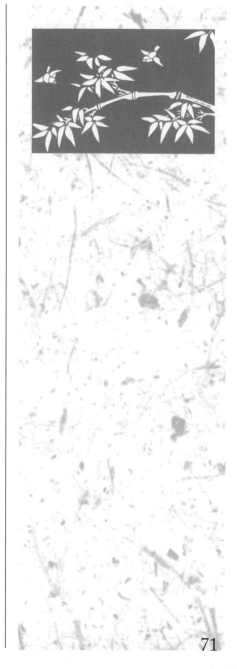

pieces directly on the oven rack. In a few minutes, they will puff up greatly and become slightly browned and cracked. (Kids love to watch this.) Flip them over and cook until the other side puffs up. They are now ready. You can also achieve the same results in a broiler. Place the pieces under your broiler until completely puffed up on one side, then flip over and broil until puffy.

Put 2 to 3 pieces of mochi in each person's bowl. Place some spinach in each bowl. Pour the hot stew into each bowl, and top with chopped scallions. Devour immediately! Chew your mochi well so that you don't choke!

Cooking With Tofu

In America, plain tofu is often considered bland, and thus by its nature is capable of absorbing the flavors of other ingredients used with it in a dish. In Japan, however, plain tofu itself is appreciated, its flavor is considered delicate rather than bland. This is especially true of tofu freshly made by neighborhood tofu shops. The Japanese tend not to doctor it up, but enjoy it in its simplicity, perhaps with a dash of soy sauce and a grating of fresh ginger, as you will see in the following recipes. Mashing tofu into burgers or blending it for sauces and desserts, as is done in modern American vegetarian recipes, are techniques that are alien to the Japanese as of yet.

Tofu in Hot Water

Yu-Dofu

3-inch piece konbu

1 quart water

1 pound very fresh tofu

Soy sauce, grated fresh ginger, and chopped
  green onions for dipping

Place the konbu and water in a pot. Bring to a
simmer.

Cut the tofu into 1-inch cubes. Place in the
water and simmer gently for two minutes. Do
not over-cook; this will toughen the tofu.
Remove from the heat. Each person then
removes cubes of tofu and dips them in either
soy sauce with a little grated ginger and green
onions or in the citrus sauce below and eats it
along with bites of rice.

Citrus Sauce (Ponzu)

3 tablespoons soy sauce

3 tablespoons lime or lemon juice

1½ tablespoons FruitSource, sugar, evaporated
  cane juice, or fructose

Combine all the ingredients and stir well to dissolve the sweetener.

*This is perhaps the most basic
way of serving tofu. Despite
its simplicity, it can be delicious
and quite warming on a cold
winter evening.*

*You will find subtle (or even
great) differences in the flavor of
tofu made by different
manufacturers. Sample several
different ones and select the
freshest tasting tofu for this and
other tofu recipes.*

Yield: 4 servings

One October day in San Francisco, we were enjoying a warm Indian summer. All of a sudden, a giant earthquake occurred (the earthquake of '89). That evening, I had a house full of people who were not able to return across the bay to their homes, as well as neighbors who had nothing to eat due to the lack of electricity and gas. Fortunately, I happened to have several pounds of freshly made tofu in my refrigerator which would have gone bad if we did not eat it right away. I served it hiya-yakko style with soy sauce and freshly grated ginger, and immediately had a houseful of converts.

Yield: 4 servings

Cold Tofu

Hiya-Yakko

This is the summertime version of Yu-Dofu (Tofu in Hot Water), page 73. Once again, only the freshest tofu is used. Silken tofu is often preferred to regular tofu for serving it in this manner, since it is more delicate.

1 pound very fresh tofu

Chopped green onions, about 1 to 2 tablespoons per person

Freshly grated ginger, about ½ teaspoon per person

Soy sauce

The tofu should be chilled. Cut it into small cubes, and top with onions and ginger. Pour a dash of soy sauce on top, and enjoy with rice on a hot summer day.

Tofu with An Sauce

Tofu no Ankake

- 2 teaspoons dark sesame oil
- ¼ pound button mushrooms, sliced
- 2 cups *Konbu to Shiitake no Dashi* (Konbu-Shiitake Stock), page 54 or *Shiitake no Dashi* (Shiitake Stock), page 55
- 3½ ounces enoki mushrooms, separated into small clumps
- 3 to 4 fresh or dried and reconstituted shiitake mushrooms, sliced
- 2 to 4 tablespoons soy sauce
- 4 tablespoons cornstarch or kuzu, dissolved in a little water
- 1 pound tofu
- Small pot of water

To make the *an* sauce, heat the sesame oil in a heavy-bottom pot. Sauté the button mushrooms for 2 minutes. Add the stock, enoki, shiitake, and soy sauce, and bring to a simmer. Simmer gently for five minutes. Slowly pour in the dissolved cornstarch, and stir until thick and clear. Season to taste with soy sauce and more sesame oil, if desired.

Cut the tofu into four slices (1 per person). Bring a pot of water to a gentle simmer. Place the tofu slices in it, and simmer gently for 2 to 3 minutes. Drain the tofu on paper towels and pat dry.

Place the tofu on individual plates or dishes. Pour some *an* sauce on each slice, and serve immediately.

Ankake is a simple sauce that is made by thickening a flavorful broth with a little kuzu or cornstarch. It is then poured over tofu, vegetables, rice, or noodles. Here is a recipe that features mushrooms.

Yield: 4 servings

75

Here is a simple dish that my mother used to frequently make for me. The sweetness of carrots plays nicely in this dish.

Carrot and Tofu Scramble
Iri-Dofu to Ninjin

1 pound firm tofu
2 tablespoons oil
1 pound carrots, grated (about 5 medium)
⅓ cup soy sauce
¼ cup sesame seeds (optional)
1 teaspoon dark sesame oil

If you are using soft tofu (as opposed to firm), wrap it in a towel and place it in the refrigerator overnight or for several hours to drain.

Crumble the tofu with your hands into little bits. In a skillet, heat the 2 tablespoons of oil and add the carrots. Sauté until fairly tender. Add the tofu and sauté until the carrots are soft and the tofu is dry. Add the soy sauce and sesame seeds, and sauté for a moment more. Finally, add the sesame oil. This is very good served with rice.

Yield: 4 servings

Tofu Steak

1 pound extra-firm tofu, cut into 4 slices about ½ inch thick

⅓ cup soy sauce

2 to 3 cloves garlic, crushed or put through a press

2 teaspoons sesame oil

1 tablespoon sake

2 tablespoons mirin

Oil or non-stick cooking spray

A slightly Western approach to tofu cuisine, different forms of "tofu steak" are being enjoyed by Japanese today.

If you are using soft tofu (as opposed to firm), wrap it in a towel and drain in the refrigerator for several hours or overnight.

Combine the soy sauce, garlic, sesame oil, sake and mirin in a bowl, and marinate the tofu in it, basting occasionally, for at least 1 hour (2 to 3 hours is preferable). Heat a little oil or nonstick spray in a skillet. Add the tofu slices and grill on each side until browned. Remove from the skillet, and serve as is, or dilute the marinade with a little water to reduce the saltiness, heat in the skillet, and pour over each "steak."

Yield: 4 servings

Tofu in a crispy coating is seasoned with teriyaki sauce.

Tofu with Teriyaki Sauce
Teriyaki Dofu

1 pound firm tofu, sliced into 4 pieces about
 ½ inch thick

Cornstarch for coating tofu

3 to 4 tablespoons oil

4 tablespoons soy sauce

3 tablespoons mirin

1 to 2 tablespoons FruitSource, sugar, evaporated
 cane juice, or light maple syrup

2 tablespoons chopped green onions

Coat the tofu slices generously with cornstarch. In a small skillet, heat the oil and fry the tofu slices in it until browned on both sides. Pour out any remaining oil. In the same skillet, combine the soy sauce, mirin, and sweetener, and bring to a boil. Turn off the heat. Toss the tofu in this sauce to coat, and then remove from the pan. Serve immediately.

Yield: 4 servings

Sautéed Tofu Wrapped in Nori

Tofu no Isobe Maki

1 pound firm tofu

4 sheets nori, preferably not toasted

1 tablespoon oil

3 tablespoons mirin

3 tablespoons soy sauce

2 teaspoons freshly grated ginger

2 to 3 scallions, minced

Cut the tofu into sticks about 1½ to 2 inches long and ½ inch thick. Wrap the tofu in pieces of nori large enough to go around them completely. If the nori is extremely crispy, allow the moisture from the tofu to soften before attempting to wrap.

Heat the oil in a frying pan. Over medium low heat, cook the tofu pieces on all sides until the nori is crispy. Combine the mirin with the soy sauce, and pour over the tofu pieces on individual plates. Top with the ginger and green onions.

Quickly prepared, the nori lends this dish a flavor from the sea.

Yield: 4 servings

This is a very loosely constructed recipe, since almost any combination of seasonal vegetables can be served this way with an sauce, a simple glaze sauce thickened with cornstarch, kuzu, or arrowroot. When this is served over rice, it becomes ankake (an poured over something). Very simple to make, this is a one-bowl meal.

This recipe is great for using up whatever vegetables you may find around the house. You can use just about any kind of leafy green or nonroot vegetable, except for tomatoes or avocados.

Yield: 4 servings

Vegetables and Tofu in An Sauce over Rice
Yasai to Tofu no Ankake

1 to 2 tablespoons oil for sautéing, or ½ cup water for steam-frying

About 6 cups of chopped or sliced vegetables, such as: cabbage, *nira* (a chive-like vegetable with a garlicky flavor), mushrooms, carrots, broccoli, bok choy, green onions, or zucchini

2 cups *Konbu Dashi* (Konbu, or Konbu-Shiitake Stock), page 54

¾ pound firm silken tofu, cut into ½-inch cubes

2 tablespoons soy sauce

2 tablespoons sake

1 teaspoon fresh grated ginger (optional)

2 to 3 tablespoons cornstarch or arrowroot, or slightly less kuzu, dissolved in 3 to 4 tablespoons water

1 teaspoon sesame oil

Heat a wok or frying pan until hot. Add the oil or the water, and let it heat for a moment. Add the vegetables, firmer ones first, and sauté or steam-fry over high heat until fairly tender. Add the stock, tofu, soy sauce, and sake, and cook until tender. Add the ginger and the dissolved cornstarch, to the pan, stirring until thickened and glossy. Turn off the heat and stir in the sesame oil. Serve over large bowls of hot rice.

Fried Tofu Dumplings

Hirosu

4 taro roots

8 ounces regular tofu, drained in paper towels for 30 minutes

2 shiitake mushrooms, minced

¼ carrot, minced

½ teaspoon sea salt

1 tablespoon flour

Flour for coating

Oil for frying

Approximately ¼ cup *daikon-oroshi* (grated daikon radish)

Soy sauce, to taste

Peel and simmer the taro root until tender, about 10 minutes. Drain, place in a bowl, and mash well. Add the tofu, mash, and mix well. Mix in the shiitake, carrot, sea salt, and the 1 tablespoon of flour. Form into little balls the size of ping-pong balls, and coat in more flour. Heat the oil until a little piece of dumpling dropped in rises steadily and quickly to the surface. Fry a few balls at a time until golden brown, turning once or twice. Drain on paper towels. Serve 2 to 4 balls per person, topped with a little grated daikon radish and soy sauce.

These delicately textured and flavored dumplings can be served as is or simmered in dashi (stock) and seasonings.

Yield: 3 to 4 servings

These are fun to make and very tasty. Differing in texture from frozen tofu one might make at home, this has a much finer, spongier consistency and absorbs flavors well. Highly versatile, this is the most traditional way of cooking koya dofu.

Freeze-Dried Tofu
Koya Dofu

1 box (approximately 3.5 ounces) *koya-dofu* (freeze dried tofu)

2 cups *dashi* (stock)

3 tablespoons soy sauce

2 tablespoons mirin

2 tablespoons sake

Reconstitute the koya dofu by soaking it in tepid water for 10 to 15 minutes. Press each piece between the palms of your hands, squeezing out the water. In a pot, combine the dashi (stock) with the soy sauce, mirin, and sake. Add the *koya dofu* (freeze dried tofu), cover partially, and simmer gently for 15 to 20 minutes, until it turns a light tan color and the flavors have been absorbed. It can be eaten as is, added to udon or soba noodles, or used as an addition to a *nabe* dish.

Yield: 4 servings

Fried Dishes

In this age of fat-free consciousness, fried dishes are taboo. However, the Japanese believe that there is a place for them. Of course, the traditional Japanese diet is overall much lower in fat than the American diet. When fried foods are served, they are offered in much smaller quantities—usually two to three morsels to round out a meal, the rest of which would most likely be fat-free. The exception is perhaps tempura, which is by far the most famous fried dish from Japan. Anyone who has enjoyed it prepared well will understand how it can constitute an entire meal. There are others, too, such as *tonkatsu*, or deep-fried pork, and *kushi-age*, deep-fried, breaded skewers of various vegetables, meat, and seafood. Here, however, we will introduce simply a handful of tasty morsels for those who would like a small, albeit rich, addition to their meal.

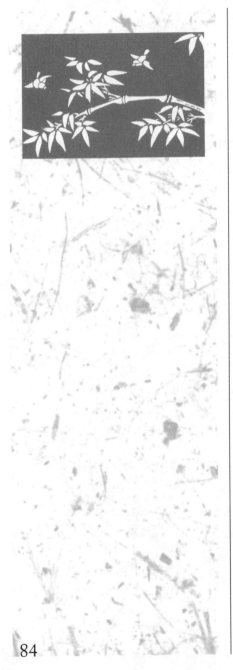

Fried Natto

Natto-Age

Two 3-ounce packages natto
3 green onions, thinly sliced
3 tablespoons cornstarch
2 teaspoons soy sauce
1 to 2 teaspoons Japanese hot mustard
2 sheets nori
Oil for frying

Mix the natto with the onions, cornstarch, soy sauce, and hot mustard. Cut the sheets of nori into eight squares each. On each square, place a small mound of the natto mixture—it will be sticky enough to adhere. Fill a fryer with oil or place at least an inch of oil in a deep skillet. Heat until a tiny bit of the mixture dropped in rises to the surface of the oil steadily and quickly. Without crowding the pan, fry a few pieces of natto-covered nori at a time until crispy and brown. Drain on absorbent paper. Serve with soy sauce and additional hot mustard for dipping.

Natto is a fermented soybean product towards which people generally have a strong liking or disliking. Whereas people from Kanto, or the Tokyo area, tend to enjoy it, those from Kansai or the Osaka area often do not. It has a strong odor, somewhat reminiscent of limburger cheese, and a sticky, stretchy consistency that many object to. (It forms "threads," they say.) I, for one, love it, as do my children. Frying it, however, rids it of most of what some consider an objectionable smell and texture, and yields a crispy, tasty product.

Yield: 4 to 6 servings

85

Dengaku is a sweet miso sauce that is served with a variety of foods, such as broiled tofu, konnyaku (page 25), and this wonderful deep-fried eggplant, another favorite dish that I tend to break down in front of. If you are trying to avoid deep-frying, the eggplants can be lightly brushed with oil and grilled or roasted until tender.

Yield: 4 to 8 servings

Fried Eggplant with Miso Sauce

Nasu no Dengaku

4 Japanese eggplants
Oil for frying or grilling

Dengaku (Sweet Miso Sauce)
⅓ cup mild white miso
2 tablespoons mirin
3 tablespoons sugar, or 3 to 4 tablespoons FruitSource or evaporated cane juice (Fruit juice concentrate does not work well here.)

Cut the eggplants in half lengthwise. Heat the oil to 375°F, or until the eggplants dropped in the hot oil first sink but fairly rapidly float to the surface. Fry until golden brown, then drain on absorbent paper. (Alternatively, the cut-side of the eggplants can be brushed lightly with oil and grilled on a hibachi or barbeque grill, or under a broiler until tender.) Mix the remaining ingredients to make the *dengaku* (sweet miso sauce), and spread on top of each eggplant. Serve immediately.

Vegetarian Calamari

Ika-Age

One 8 to 10 ounce package white konnyaku, page 25 (grey can be used, but the white looks more convincing)

Flour for dredging

Oil for frying

Salt, lemon juice, *ponzu* (light, salty, citrus dipping sauce), or soy sauce to taste

Slice the konnyaku ¼ inch thick. Dredge well in flour. Heat the oil until a small piece of konnyaku dropped in rises steadily and quickly to the surface. Fry several pieces at a time until crispy and light brown. Drain well. Serve with lemon juice, sea salt, *ponzu* (light, salty, citrus dipping sauce), or soy sauce, if desired.

Konnyaku may seem rubbery and strange, but I have found that it makes an excellent substitute for calamari. It has a fishy enough flavor, and the texture is perfect.

Yield: 2 to 4 servings

Delicate silken tofu morsels with a crisp "skin" in a savory broth—this happens to be another one of my favorites. Unfortunately, these really do have to be fried, not baked.

Deep-Fried Tofu in Broth
Age-Dashi Dofu

3 cups *Konbu to Shiitake no Dashi* (Konbu-Shiitake Stock), page 54 or *Shiitake no Dashi* (Shiitake Stock), page 55

2 to 3 tablespoons soy sauce

½ teaspoon sea salt

2 tablespoons sake

1 tablespoon mirin

¼ pound daikon radish, peeled

Oil for frying

1½ pounds firm silken tofu, cut into 1-inch cubes

About ½ cup cornstarch

2 teaspoons grated fresh ginger

3 green onions, chopped or thinly sliced

Combine the stock with the soy sauce, sea salt, sake, and mirin, and simmer for 5 minutes. Grate the daikon with a Japanese grater or the finest grate on an American grater. Set aside a little for topping, and gently squeeze out the excess water from the rest. (You will end up with only about ¼ cup of daikon.) Heat the oil for frying, and coat each cube of tofu well in the cornstarch. Fry several cubes at a time until golden, then drain on absorbent paper.

Put several cubes in each person's bowl, and pour over ½ cup of the sauce per serving. Top with a little grated daikon, ginger, and green onion, and serve immediately.

Yield: 6 servings

Fried Tofu with Mushrooms
Kinoko no Age-Dashi Dofu

Prepare Age-Dashi Dofu (opposite page) with the following changes:

If desired, delete the daikon and ginger.

To the broth, add:

A slightly more elaborate version of Age-Dashi Dofu with the addition of Japanese mushrooms.

3 ounces each enoki and *shimeji* (oyster mushrooms), separated into small clumps or individual mushrooms (Thinly sliced shiitake mushrooms can be substituted if enokis and oysters are unavailable.)

Simmer for 7 to 8 minutes. Chives or green onions can be added for a light flavor and garnish.

Yield: 6 servings

89

This famous and wonderful Japanese dish, like sushi, is so highly regarded by the Japanese that people rarely make it at home, leaving it to highly skilled chefs at tempura restaurants. Very good tempura can be expensive, too, but so delicate, light, and tasty that one finds it difficult to believe that it is just vegetables with batter. In no way does it taste like onion rings.

Yield: 4 to 6 servings

Vegetable Tempura
Yasai Tempura

Oil for deep-frying (can be part sesame oil)

Various vegetables of choice
Thinly sliced onions
Whole or halved mushrooms
Broccoli flowers
Zucchini sliced diagonally ⅓ inch thick
Slices of sweet potato
Slices of kabocha or butternut squash
Parsley
Shiitake
Slices of eggplant
String beans
Asparagus spears
Very thin carrot sticks (almost slivers)

Batter
1 cup whole wheat pastry flour or unbleached pastry or all-purpose white flour
2 tablespoons cornstarch
A pinch of baking soda
1 cup ice water

Ten-Tsuyu (Tempura Sauce)
1½ cups *Konbu Dashi* (Konbu or Konbu-Shiitake Stock), page 54
½ to ⅔ cup soy sauce
¼ cup mirin
Grated fresh ginger and/or daikon (optional)

The three important points to remember are:

1. Mix the batter ever so lightly;
2. Have the oil at the proper temperature;
3. Never crowd the fryer.

Have all your ingredients ready before you begin frying so that you can dip, fry, and drain quickly and systematically. For deep-frying, refined oil usually work best. Never reuse frying oil as it not only imparts an unpleasant flavor but is not good for one's health.

Wash and drain or dry the vegetables and cut them into sizes that can be eaten in 2 to 3 bites. Onions and carrots are usually combined with the last of the batter and fried in clumps, so save them for last. Have all the vegetables ready for dipping and frying.

Start heating the oil to around 350°F. Mix the flour, cornstarch, baking soda, and water gently, leaving in some of the lumps and making sure that you do not over mix it. Test the oil for fry-ing—a small bit of batter dropped in the oil should sink and rise to the surface fairly quickly. If the batter sinks and does not rise, or rises very slowly, the oil is not hot enough. If it hardly sinks before sizzling at the surface, the oil is too hot. Dip the vegetables in the batter one piece at

Tempura is a perfect balance of vegetables coated with just the right amount of batter and deep-fried to a light, crispy perfection. It is then dipped in a soy-based sauce and eaten together with rice. Altogether, it can be a heavenly experience. On the other hand, bad tempura will usually have more batter than the star ingredient inside and be oily and soggy. It is all in the technique of preparation and cooking, and can be duplicated at home once a few tricks are mastered.

a time, and fry immediately. Do not fry any more vegetables at one time than will cover half the surface of the oil or the temperature of the oil may drop, and you will end up with soggy pieces of tempura. Fry until golden brown, about 1 to 2 minutes. Remove and drain and continue with the remaining vegetables, mixing up more batter if necessary. Onion slices and thin carrot sticks can be combined with the last of the batter and be fried in clumps.

While the vegetables are frying, combine the stock, soy sauce, and mirin, and heat until boiling. Turn down the heat and simmer gently for 2 or 3 minutes.

To serve, pour about a third of a cup of the tempura sauce in individual bowls. A little grated ginger or daikon may be added at this time if desired—remove excess water first by wringing with your hands. Dip the tempura vegetables in the sauce and enjoy with rice.

"Fishy" Tempura Tempeh

8 ounces tempeh
⅓ cup soy sauce
2 sheets nori
Tempura batter
Oil for frying

Cut the tempeh into ¼-inch strips and marinate in the soy sauce for at least 20 minutes. Cut the nori into pieces as long as the tempeh strips and wide enough to wrap around them completely with a little extra for overlap. Wrap each tempeh strip in the nori, using a dab or two of the tempura batter to "glue" the nori in place. Dip each piece of nori-wrapped tempeh in the tempura batter and deep fry in oil at 375°F until golden brown and crispy. Drain on paper towels and serve immediately.

Here is an idea for tempura that adds substance, texture, and variety to a platter of vegetable tempura. Tempeh strips are wrapped in nori, dipped in tempura batter, and fried until crispy. The result is a meaty substance with flavors of the sea —a great vegan addition to tempura veggies. If you tell someone from Japan what you're eating, however, they will be baffled, since tempeh is not found in Japan.

Yield: 3 to 4 servings

93

A medley of thinly slivered vegetables, primarily root vegetables, are held together by tempura batter and deep-fried into little cakes. This allows the cook to vary the medley with different vegetable combinations, as well as "season" it by adding ingredients such as slivered shiso leaves, nori, or sesame seeds. Although here I describe more of a method rather than an exact recipe, the important point is not to use too much batter or to overmix. Over-handling will yield a heavy cake with lots of doughy batter. Be light-handed with both the amount of tempura batter you mix in and how you combine it with the vegetables.

Tempura of Julienne Vegetables

Kaki-Age

1 cup thinly sliced onions
1 cup julienne (slivered) carrots
About 2 cups more vegetables, cut julienne or slivered (zucchini, broccoli stalks, asparagus, sweet potato, shiitake mushrooms, etc.)
Slivered nori or shiso leaves (optional)
Pinch baking soda
1¼ cups all-purpose or cake flour
1¼ cups ice water
Oil for frying

Prepare the vegetables, cutting them as thinly as possible into slivers or julienne. Combine in a bowl. In another bowl, mix the baking soda into the flour, and make a well in the center. Pour in the ice water, and combine rapidly to mix; do not worry about lumps. Pour over the vegetable mixture, and mix gently and quickly. Do not over mix.

Heat the oil in a wok fryer to 375°F, or until a piece of vegetable floats steadily but immediately to the top. Depending on the size of the frying utensil, drop in the mixture by the half-cupful or so, making sure that no more than half of the surface is covered. With a pair of chopsticks, quickly spread out the mixture slightly and gently in the oil, so that it does not make too thick of a cake. Fry to a golden brown, turning once. Drain well. Serve with *Ten-Tsuyu* (Tempura Sauce), pages 90-92.

Crispy Fried Tempeh
Kara-Age Tempeh

8 ounces tempeh or "chicken-flavored" seitan

⅓ cup soy sauce

1 clove garlic, minced

1 tablespoon mirin (optional)

Cornstarch or arrowroot for coating

Oil for frying

Karashi (Japanese hot mustard) (optional)

Soy sauce (optional)

Slice the tempeh ⅓-inch thick. Combine the soy sauce with the garlic and optional mirin, and marinate the tempeh in it for at least 20 minutes. Remove the tempeh and drain. Heat the oil until a little piece of tempeh dropped in rises quickly to the top, about 375°F. Coat each piece of tempeh in cornstarch, and fry in the oil until golden brown and crispy. Drain on paper towels and serve immediately as is or with a little karashi and shoyu.

Kara-age is actually a method of frying rather than a particular recipe. The item to be fried—usually chicken, fish, or vegetables—is coated with cornstarch or flour and deep-fried until crispy. In my family, kara-age chicken was a favorite (until I became a vegetarian at age 12, of course, although the rest of my family continued to eat it). Although tempeh is not a Japanese food (it is not even sold there), I find that it makes a tasty substitute for chicken. If desired, "chicken-style" seitan sold in stores can be prepared the same way.

Yield: 3 to 4 servings

95

Salads and Cold Vegetables

The Japanese frequently prepare cooked vegetables in a fashion that can be enjoyed cold. Along with some traditional preparations, I have introduced a few more recent concoctions on the order of salads with dressings.

Spinach with Sesame Sauce

Horenso no Goma-Ae

2 medium bunches spinach, thoroughly rinsed in water until no trace of sand or dirt remains (Try to keep the bunches together.)

⅓ cup white sesame seeds

2 to 3 tablespoons granulated cane juice, FruitSource, brown rice syrup, or sugar

¼ cup soy sauce

Fill a large pot with water, and bring to a boil. Add the spinach, and cook only for a minute, just until the spinach wilts. Do not overcook! (The spinach can be steamed, although this is not the traditional manner of preparation.) Holding the bunch neatly, run under cold water until thoroughly cool, then squeeze well to remove the excess water. Place on a cutting board, and cut into 1-inch lengths. Place in an attractive dish or bowl.

In a small skillet, toast the sesame seeds over medium heat until they make a crackling sound. Remove immediately; do not allow them to color or burn, as this renders a bitter flavor. Place the sesame seeds in a suribachi, a mortar, or a blender. If using a suribachi or mortar, grind and pound the sesame seeds with the pestle until they begin to release oil, but stop short of producing a paste or butter. If using a blender, grind them briefly until they begin to look oily, but do not over blend. Add the sweetener and soy sauce, mix well, and pour over the spinach.

This is one of my favorite ways to serve spinach. It happens to be a hit with my young son, too, who usually has to grin and bear his veggies. Ideally, the simple sauce is best ground in a Japanese suri-bachi, a mortar with grooves. It can, however, be made in a blender if one is very careful not to overblend. If the sesame seeds are blended too long, they will turn into sesame butter.

Yield: 4 servings as a side dish

97

Blanched Spinach or Greens
Horenso no Hitashi

1 bunch spinach, kale, mustard greens, chard, or if available, komatsu-na or shun-giku
Soy sauce

This is a basic method of preparing leafy greens that can be served cold or at room temperature. Most frequently, spinach or a spinach-like vegetable called komatsu-na are used, but greens more commonly found in the United States, such as kale or mustard greens, can be used as well. The preparation is extremely simple and the flavor very clean.

Wash the vegetables thoroughly. In Japan where aesthetics mean almost everything, a cook would be careful to keep all the root ends together so that after cooking, rinsing, and squeezing, the vegetables could be cut in an extremely neat fashion, with all the strands together as in a rope. Blanch the greens in the pot of boiling water just until they wilt and are tender. The amount of time will depend on the greens used; spinach will take but a moment, whereas kale will take a few minutes. Remove the greens from the water and run under cold water to stop the cooking process. Squeeze out all the liquid. Place the strand of greens on a cutting board, and cut into 1-inch segments. Place in individual bowls and serve with a little soy sauce poured on top.

Yield 2 to 6 servings

My Mother's Simple Spinach with Sesame Oil

Horenso no Goma-Abura-Ae

1 bunch spinach
2 tablespoons toasted sesame oil
Salt, to taste

This is truly a simple side dish, and yet so tasty! It is a slightly richer variation of Blanched Spinach or Greens (Horenso no Hitashi), opposite page.

Blanch, steam, or microwave the spinach until just wilted. Rinse in cold water to stop the cooking process. (It does not have to be completely cold as with *Horenso no Hitashi*.) Squeeze until fairly dry, and cut into 1-inch lengths.

In a bowl, pour in the sesame oil and a few sprinklings of sea salt. Stir to dissolve the sea salt, then add the spinach and mix well. Serve at room temperature.

Yield: 2 to 4 as a small side dish

Here is a simple dressing that contains very little fat per serving. It is tasty over regular greens, shredded cabbage (a common component of Japanese salads), reconstituted wakame, or other delicate sea vegetables. At our restaurant, Now and Zen, we serve this over our popular "Wakame Salad," which consists of romaine lettuce topped with delicate wakame, fresh corn, tomatoes, red onions, and cucumbers.

Yield: 1¾ cups

Japanese Style Salad Dressing

Wa-Fu Dressingu

Scant ½ cup soy sauce

⅓ cup fruit juice concentrate or Fruit Source, or ¼ cup sugar

¾ cup rice wine vinegar

1 tablespoon sesame oil

1 tablespoon toasted sesame seeds (optional)

Whisk all the ingredients together.

Wakame Salad

Wakame Salada

Per serving:

Approximately 1 to 2 tablespoons dried, chopped wakame soaked in ¼ cup of water,

or ¼ cup salted fresh wakame, rinsed, soaked, re-rinsed, and diced

Reconstitute the wakame in the water for 10 minutes. It will swell and and come to life. Drain.

Although packs of finely chopped, dried wakame contain only a few ounces, remember that you don't need much for your salad; about 1 to 2 tablespoons per person will reconstitute into a generous portion. Some Japanese grocery stores carry fresh wakame preserved in salt in their refrigerated section. It should look tender. Be sure to rinse it thoroughly, then soak and rinse again before using it, or you will choke on the salt.

For the salad:

Any vegetables you like: lettuce, tomatoes, cucumbers, scallions, red onions, grated carrots, fresh corn kernels, etc.

Arrange the vegetables on a plate, top with the wakame, and pour on a generous serving of Wa-Fu Dressing. Devour immediately.

Wakame salads started to appear on the Japanese culinary scene in the '80s as the Japanese began to adopt Western foods. They added soy sauce to a basic vinaigrette and made "Wa-Fu Dressing."

Then they poured it on top of tender wakame and greens, and voilà, a new culinary tradition was established. Using the most tender wakame you can find for this dish is of paramount importance. Often, you will find chopped, dried wakame marketed as "cut wakame" in Japanese food stores. Obviously tough-looking, stringy wakame in long strands will not do the job when it comes to eating it raw and fresh.

Yield: 1 serving

Here is a mayonnaise-based dressing that suits any type of greens. Feel free to use full-fat, low-fat, tofu-based, or non-fat mayo in making this. It is especially suitable for a Japanese-style cole slaw.

Creamy Japanese Dressing
Wa-Fu Mayonezu Dressingu

½ cup vegan mayonnaise
¼ cup rice vinegar
3 tablespoons sweetener of your choice
½ teaspoon sea salt
1 tablespoon soy sauce

Mix everything together well. Combine with greens of your choice.

Yield: approximately 1 cup

Miso Dressing

Miso Dressingu

2 to 3 tablespoons light miso
2 tablespoons sweetener of choice
¼ cup rice vinegar
¼ cup salad oil

Combine the miso with the sweetener. Mix in the vinegar. Whisk in the oil until emulsified.

The type of miso you use will determine exactly how much is added to this tasty dressing. A milder white or koji miso is preferable in this dressing.

Yield: ¾ cup

103

Here is an interesting salad that my mother taught me.

Cucumber and Wakame Salad with Miso Dressing

Kyuri to Wakame no Miso Dressingu Kake

2 Japanese cucumbers

¾ cup reconstituted tender wakame, lightly squeezed

½ cup *Konbu Dashi* (Konbu Stock), page 54

¼ cup white miso

2 tablespoons liquid sweetener, such as FruitSource, rice syrup, evaporated cane juice, or sugar

2 tablespoons rice vinegar, or to taste

Slice the cucumbers as thinly as possible. Combine with the wakame in a bowl. To make the dressing, heat the stock in a small pan with the miso, and simmer for 2 to 3 minutes to dissolve it completely. Add the sweetener and rice vinegar, adjusting the quantity as necessary to achieve a balance between sweetness and tartness. Allow the dressing to cool for 5 to 10 minutes. Combine with the cucumbers and chill briefly before serving.

Yield: 3 to 4 servings

Cucumber Salad with Wa-Fu Dressing

Dressing

⅓ cup rice wine vinegar

1 tablespoon soy sauce

1 to 2 tablespoons frozen apple or white grape juice concentrate, FruitSource, or sugar

½ teaspoon sea salt

1 tablespoon canola oil

Several drops sesame oil

2 Japanese cucumbers, or ½ medium European cucumber, sliced as thinly as possible (paper thin is recommended)

Whisk the dressing together and pour over the cucumbers in a bowl. Toss lightly. Serve right away or allow to marinate for 30 minutes. (This will soften the cucumber slices.)

An all-time favorite of my little daughters! They will crunch away on slice after slice of this refreshing and simple salad. It is especially good as a condiment to accompany fried dishes. Most important for the salad is the type of cucumber used. Only Japanese cucumbers or the long, thin European variety are recommended, since they are not waxed nor do they have bitter skins.

Yield: Serves 2 hungry little girls or 3 to 4 adults as a condiment/salad.

A refreshingly sweet dengaku sauce made of white miso with citrus overtones from the zest of yuzu (a Japanese citrus fruit) dresses slices of konnyaku. If yuzu is unavailable, lemon zest can be substituted, although it will have an obviously different aroma. Instead of konnyaku, Yu-Dofu (Tofu in Hot Water, page 73) can be the host for the sauce. Konnyaku served in this fashion is completely fat-free!

Yield: 4 servings

Konnyaku with Sweet Miso and Citrus Sauce

Konnyaku no Yuzu Dengaku Kake

One 8-ounce package konnyaku, white or dark
¼ cup white miso
2 tablespoons mirin
1 to 2 tablespoons evaporated cane juice, maple syrup, FruitSource, or sugar
2 tablespoons water
Grated zest of ¾ to 1 yuzu

Slice the konnyaku ¼ inch thick. Simmer in boiling water for five minutes; drain. Combine the miso with the remaining ingredients to form a thick sauce. Adjust the degree of sweetness and the amount of yuzu zest, depending on the type of sweetener you use and how fragrant with yuzu you would like the sauce to be.

Place the slices next to each other on a plate, and pour the sauce over them. Serve immediately. This can also be served at room temperature.

Mountain Yam with Plum Sauce

Nagaimo no Ume-Ae

12 ounces *naga-imo* (mountain yams), pared

2 tablespoons plum paste

2 tablespoons evaporated cane juice, or 3 tablespoons white grape juice concentrate

Slice the peeled yams into ¼-inch thick rounds, then slice the rounds diagonally to form sticks.

Combine the plum paste with the sweetener to make a sauce. Toss with the mountain yam sticks, divide among 6 small dishes, and serve immediately.

Yield: 6 servings

Noodles

O-Soba

B ecause of their ease of preparation, lightness of fare, easy digestibility, and versatility, noodles are loved by the Japanese. They are even considered to be symbolic of longevity and are eaten on New Year's Eve to ensure a long life.

S*oba* (buckwheat noodles) and *udon* (fat, white, wheat flour noodles) are the two basic forms of pasta in Japanese cuisine. Within these two broad categories are many variations, such as *cha-soba*, buckwheat noodles with green tea added, *somen*, a type of white angel hair pasta always served icy cold with a dipping sauce, or *kishimen*, a broad, flat wheat noodle. Both soba and udon can be served hot or cold, depending on the season.

By emulating the cholesterol- and fat-laden foods served by fast food restaurants in America, the Japanese have developed a concept that surpasses these in both speed and nutrition: *tachi-gui soba* stands (literally "stand-and-eat" soba stands). These are prevalent in and near every train station or wherever people may be in a hurry to down a bowl of something light yet healthful. In contrast, there are soba or udon restaurants that take the art of noodle making to its zenith. Flour is often ground on the premises and the noodles made by hand by a master noodle maker who often rolls and cuts his pasta in a window visible to passersby. These noodles have a wonderful flavor and texture, a "slippery" quality great for slurping. I know of two restaurants in Tokyo that serve the finest bowls of soba I have ever tasted. Each time I return to Japan, I go out of my way to schedule a trip to them, despite their cost. A diner is served a large bowl with hardly enough soba to satisfy—two or three slurps and it's gone.

Either soba or udon can be used in any of the following dishes. To cook soba or udon, follow the package instructions. (Times may vary for each manufacturer.) *Soba-yu*, the water used to boil buckwheat noodles, is considered very healthful and is often served at the end of the meal to dilute the remaining soba broth, and then it is drunk. (This does not apply to udon.)

This recipe is for hot soba or udon. The noodles are served in a large bowl of broth and slurped loudly. According to Japanese noodle-eating etiquette, it is believed that a diner must slurp noisily or he cannot possibly enjoy the fullness of the dish. If you eat too quietly, you might be suspected of being a foreigner!

Yield: 4 servings

Soba or Udon in Broth
Kake-Soba or Udon

Basic Broth for Soba or Udon
(Soba or Udon Tsuyu)

3 cups *Konbu Dashi* (Konbu or Konbu-Shiitake Stock), page 54

¼ to ½ teaspoon salt

2 to 4 tablespoons soy sauce (preferably usu-kuchi)

2 tablespoons sake

1 teaspoon mirin

12 to 16 ounces soba or udon cooked according to package instructions and drained

Simmer everything but the noodles for 5 to 6 minutes. Pour over drained, hot noodles in four deep bowls. Top with chopped green onions if desired.

Food is generally saltier the farther north one travels in Japan. Thus, broths and sauces in Tokyo generally have a higher salt or soy sauce content than the equivalent in Osaka. In the following recipes, vary the amount of soy sauce or salt to suit your taste.

Tempura Soba or Udon

Tempura Soba or Udon

One of the tastiest ways to serve either soba or udon.

1 recipe *Soba or Udon Tsuyu* (Basic Broth for Soba or Udon), page 110

12 to 16 ounces dry soba or udon, cooked and drained

12 to 16 pieces tempura (pages 90-92), or 4 pieces *kaki-age* (mixed vegetable tempura)

Pour the broth over the noodles in bowls, and top with tempura. Serve immediately.

Wakame Soba or Udon

Wakame also makes a delightful topping for bowls of soba or udon. On top of each steaming bowl of *kake-soba* (soba or udon in broth) place a handful of chopped, reconstituted wakame.

Yield: 4 servings

Abura-age (fried tofu pouches) are cooked, seasoned, and placed atop steaming bowls of soba or udon. A favorite with children.

The Fox's Favorite Soba or Udon

Kitsune Soba or Udon

1 recipe Basic Broth for Soba or Udon, page 110

½ cup *Konbu Dashi* (Konbu or Konbu-Shiitake Stock), page 54

2 to 3 tablespoons soy sauce

1 to 2 tablespoons FruitSource or sugar, or 3 tablespoons mirin

4 pieces *abura-age* (fried tofu pouches), cut in quarters or halves

Place all the ingredients in a small pot. Cover tightly with a lid, and simmer for about 15 minutes, or until the pieces of *abura-age* (fried tofu pouches) have softened, darkened, and absorbed the flavors. Place the age on top of each serving of basic soba or udon.

Yield: 4 servings

Curry Udon

Karei Udon

4 tablespoons oil

½ cup plus 2 tablespoons flour

1 to 2 tablespoons curry powder (depending on the type and degree of heat desired)

5 cups hot vegetable or mushroom stock

4 tablespoons soy sauce

2 teaspoons maple syrup or other sweetener, to round out the flavor (optional)

8 to 10 ounces udon noodles, or 4 bundles

Water for boiling the udon noodles

3 to 4 scallions, chopped (optional)

In a 2-quart saucepan, heat the oil. Add the flour and cook, stirring for a minute over low heat. Add the curry powder and cook another minute. Whisk in the hot vegetable stock all at once; it will thicken almost instantaneously. (If you have not heated the stock, add it a little at a time, whisking after each addition to prevent lumps.) Add the soy sauce and sweetener, and cook until thick enough to coat the back of a wooden spoon.

Meanwhile, cook the udon in a large pot of boiling water. When al dente, drain well, rinse, and place into 4 large bowls. Fill each bowl with curry sauce, top with scallions, and serve immediately.

My mother frequently made the instant kind of curry udon (like instant ramen) for me when I came home from from grade school. It was very comforting and satisfying—a big bowl of fat udon noodles swimming in a thick, curry broth—yet the mild spiciness was quite titillating to me as a child.

Yield: 4 servings

113

Ramen

Ramen is absolutely cult food in Japan. People worship it; conversations center on where the best ramen shop is. Television shows feature the best ramen shops in every metropolis. Popular ramen shops will often have a line out the door and around the corner. It is considered the great all-time midnight snack. I remember one ramen stall (a permanent one that opened to the sidewalk and had no seats or tables) in a section of Tokyo called Ebisu that opened for only three hours each evening from 9:30 to 12:30. Apparently, the ramen there was excellent, and the sidewalk was packed each evening with connoisseurs standing in the dark, noisily slurping down their bowls of ramen. Juzo Itami, a Japanese movie director, made an outrageously funny comedy called *Tampopo* about the search for the perfect bowl of ramen, complete with tips on the etiquette of eating it properly.

Ordering in a ramen shop offers the diner several choices. Traditionally, there are three types of soup bases for ramen: *shio-aji* (salt flavor), *shoyu-aji* (soy sauce flavor), and *miso-aji* (miso flavor). In addition, there are various toppings for noodles, including sautéed bean sprouts, smoked pork slices, corn, butter, mixed vegetables, and chicken. Unfortunately, all the soup stocks are typically made with pork and/or chicken, and thus the search for vegetarian ramen in Japan is virtually futile. Here at last is a vegan version with variations made easily at home.

About the noodles themselves: Try to procure fresh Chinese ramen noodles if you can; these are available at some Asian groceries. However, good dried ones exist, as well, in Asian or natural food stores. If necessary, the so-called "instant" type in packets can be used but are not generally the same quality.

Almost Instant Ramen Noodles

Ramen

3 to 3½ cups vegetable stock

3 cups sliced cabbage

2 tablespoons sake

2 tablespoons usu-kuchi soy sauce, or
   3 tablespoons regular soy sauce

6 ounces dried or fresh ramen or *chuka-soba*
   noodles (vermicelli)

6 ounces vegetarian "ground beef" or "sausage"

½ bunch scallions, chopped

2 teaspoons sesame oil, or 1 teaspoon chili
   sesame oil

Bring the vegetable stock to a boil. Add the cabbage, sake, and soy sauce, and simmer for 3 to 4 minutes. Add the noodles. If you are using dried noodles, cook for a couple of minutes, then add the "meat." If using fresh noodles, both the noodles and the "meat" can be added simultaneously. Simmer until the noodles are tender, usually another couple of minutes. If the noodles have soaked up too much liquid, add a little more broth. Add the scallions and sesame oil, divide the noodles between two large *donburi* (ramen bowls), and serve immediately.

Any number of variations are possible with this dish. Add shiitake or sliced button mushrooms, or use them in place of cabbage. If desired, two tablespoons of miso can be added to make "miso"-flavored ramen. Top with sautéed mung bean sprouts or reconstituted wakame. Nori slivers are also a good topping. Add frozen or fresh corn (off the cob) while cooking the noodles.

Yield: 2 servings

The Japanese love their noodles cold as well as hot. Slurping chilled noodles in the hot, humid months of summer when appetites have been dulled is virtually a ritual. There are numerous variations of the theme with different types of noodles, condiments, and yes— even different degrees of coldness. Zaru-soba, cold buckwheat noodles, are generally served at room temperature, while the vermicelli-like somen is always served in a bowl of ice and water. Whatever the temperature, noodles are always dipped in individual bowls of dipping sauce called tsuyu and are enjoyed to the last mouthful. Here is a recipe for o-tsuyu that works for dipping any of the noodles.

Yield: 4 servings

Various Cold Noodles

Zaru-Soba, Udon, Hiya-Mugi, or Somen

Tsuyu (Rich Dipping Broth)

1 cup *dashi* (stock)
¼ cup soy sauce
¼ cup mirin, or to taste
Condiments added to taste:
   Wasabi
   Minced scallions
   Slivered nori (optional)

Heat the *dashi* (stock), soy sauce, and mirin to a gentle simmer, cook for 5 minutes, and turn off the heat. Cool and serve with the noodle of your choice. Add the listed condiments, if desired. Hot tsuyu can also be served with cold soba or udon.

Cold Soba or Cold Udon

Zaru-Soba or Zaru Udon

Cook soba or udon according to the package instructions; do not overcook. They will have a much silkier surface for slurping if they are left al dente and are not overcooked. Rinse in plenty of cold running water, and drain thoroughly.

Place a generous mound on each plate (or, if you are fortunate enough to find them, the bamboo trays made for them), and top with slivered nori, if desired. Provide each diner with about ⅓ cup tsuyu, some wasabi, and scallions.

Tempura Soba or Udon (Cold)

Tempura is an excellent accompaniment to zaru soba or udon (cold noodles). Provide each diner with a few pieces of tempura. Both noodles and tempura are dipped in tsuyu and eaten.

Natto Soba or Udon

Natto can also be served with zaru soba or udon. Each diner can add some natto to his or her own tsuyu and dip the noodles in it. Very thinly slivered shiso leaves are excellent to add to this.

Buckwheat noodles or udon noodles are generally served cooked, rinsed, and drained—that is, at room temperature.

Whether called a nagaimo (long potato) or yamaimo (mountain yam), this tuber with its slightly hairy skin and white "meat" is thought to be full of health benefits, providing stamina and aiding digestion with its many digestive enzymes. It is always eaten raw, either grated to form a stretchy, viscous consistency (now officially referred to as tororo) or served julienne with soy sauce or some other sauce.

Yield: 1 serving

Soba with Grated Mountain Yam

Tororo Soba

Tororo

Per serving, you will need about a 2-inch-long piece of *nagaimo* (long potato), also called *yamaimo* (mountain yam). Peel the skin. With a Japanese grater or the very smallest holes of a 4-sided American-style grater, grate the potato. It will form a thick, viscous, stretchy mass.

To serve Hot Tororo Soba

Per serving:
1 to 1½ cups cooked soba noodles per bowl
1 cup hot Basic Broth for Soba or Udon (page 110)
⅓ to ½ cup tororo
1 tablespoon chopped scallions

Pour the hot broth over the noodles. Top with tororo and the scallions. Serve immediately.

To serve Chilled Tororo Soba

Per serving:

1 to 1½ cups cooked soba noodles, chilled or at room temperature (If they have stuck together slightly, rinse them under cold water and drain momentarily.)

½ cup Rich *Tsuyu* (Dipping Broth) for *Zaru-Soba* (Cold Noodles), page 116

⅓-½ cup tororo

Chopped scallions (optional)

Wasabi horseradish (optional)

Mix the tsuyu and the tororo together, or add a little tororo to your dipping sauce as you eat. You may also add scallions and a hit of wasabi if you please. Dip, slurp, and enjoy!

If the consistency of the grated vegetable does not seem appealing (although I personally love it), try just eating a crunchy, raw slice; it's not as slimy that way. (See the recipe for Mountain Yam with Plum Sauce on page 107.) With soba noodles, nagaimo is always grated into tororo. The noodles can be served either hot or cold, depending on the season.

Meals in a Pot
Nabemono

These dishes favored by the Japanese are easy to pre-pare and fun to eat. They are designed for commu-nal eating, as all the ingredients are cooked together in a large pot (usually earthenware), often at the dinner table over a flame. The hungry diners dive in together, eating the mélange of vegetables, tofu, noodles, and whatnot with their bowls of rice. Often there is a sauce for dipping.

Most of these dishes are perfect for cold wintery days, although some can be enjoyed year round. A savory broth results from cooking the cornucopia of ingredients.

Daikon, Atsu-Age and Spinach in a Miso Broth

Daikon to Atsu-Age No Nabe

Definitely cold weather food, thick slices of daikon, atsu-age (deep-fried tofu), and spinach (including the rosy end of the spinach stem usually discarded, but very sweet) are featured in this savory one-pot dish. Atsu-age (deep fried tofu) is available in Japanese markets.

1 large daikon radish (approximately 2 pounds)

4 cups *Konbu Dashi* (Konbu Stock), page 54

2 to 3 tablespoons miso

2 to 3 tablespoons soy sauce

12 ounces *atsu-age* (deep fried tofu), cut either into triangles with 1½-inch sides or 1-inch cubes

12 ounces fresh spinach

2 teaspoons sesame oil

Peel the daikon and cut it into 1-inch circles. Cut each circle in half to form semi-circles. Place in a pot with the dashi, cover, and simmer for 30 minutes. Add the miso, soy sauce, and *atsu-age* (deep-fried tofu), and simmer for another 15 minutes. The daikon should be very tender.

Clean the spinach thoroughly and trim the bottoms but do not throw them away; these will be used in the stew, as well, to add a little pink color and sweet flavor. Add the spinach bottoms, cook for a minute, then add the leaves and simmer until just wilted. Remove from the heat and add the sesame oil. Serve immediately with hot steamed rice.

Yield: 4 to 6 servings

Some of you may remember a pop tune called the "Sukiyaki Song" that hit the airwaves here some years ago. Whether or not you understood what sukiyaki was from the song, you will understand after tasting this why sukiyaki is so popular in Japan, as well as in Japanese restaurants here in the States.

Yield: 6 servings

Sukiyaki

Sukiyaki

2 tablespoons oil (optional)

1 pound firm tofu, sliced ⅓ inch thick

½ pound seitan, sliced as thinly as possible (¼ inch thick or less) (optional)

¾ pound mushrooms, preferably some or all fresh shiitake mushrooms and enoki or *shimeji* (oyster mushrooms)

½ kabocha or butternut squash, cut into ⅓-inch slices

2 zucchinis, thickly sliced, or ½ bunch broccoli, cut into spears

1 pound shirataki noodles (sometimes referred to as konnyaku noodles)

1 cup soy sauce

½ cup granulated sugar, FruitSource, or ¾ cup brown rice syrup

⅓ cup mirin

6 cups roughly cut napa cabbage, mustard greens, or kale

4 bunches green onions, cut into 3-inch lengths

4 cups mung bean sprouts (optional)

1 to 2 teaspoons grated fresh ginger (optional)

Heat the oil in a deep, large skillet, and sauté the tofu and seitan on both sides until browned. Push the tofu and seitan over to one side of the

pan, add the mushrooms, and sauté for another minute until browned. (These steps can be omitted if you would like to eliminate the oil. Simply place the tofu and seitan in the skillet, and follow the rest of the recipe).

Push the mushrooms to another part of the skillet, then add the squash, zucchini, and shirataki noodles, separately and in neat piles in the skillet. Combine the soy sauce, sweetener of choice, and mirin, and add to the skillet. When the contents have come to a boil, turn down the heat to a gentle simmer. Add the greens, green onions, and bean sprouts, all in separate piles, and continue simmering for a few minutes until the vegetables are tender. Add the ginger, cook another moment, then taste. If the broth is too salty, add some water. (The vegetables themselves will exude water; thus, the additional water is a matter of taste).

Each diner helps himself to the delectables in the skillet, eating them with an ample supply of rice. It should be noted that the sodium content is not as frightfully high as it would seem, since most of the liquid in the pot is not consumed.

Ideally, this would be cooked at the table in an electric skillet. Have a heaping plate of additional vegetables and other ingredients that can be added to the skillet and cooked as the delectable ingredients in it are consumed. Vegetables other than those suggested here can be substituted. Shirataki or konnyaku noodles are truly calorie-free noodles made from a special mountain yam and are available in the refrigerated section of Japanese grocery stores.

Stewed and Braised Dishes

In these mostly vegetable dishes, the flavors penetrate the vegetables, and the dish can be served either hot or cold. The amount of soy sauce and sweetener used varies greatly with the household as well as the region; Tokyo cooks tend to go a little more heavily on the soy sauce than their Kyoto or Osaka counterparts who prefer a lighter flavor. You may adjust the seasonings to your own taste.

Stewed Vegetables

Ni-Mono

Root vegetables of choice:

4 to 6 cups large bite-sized pieces peeled carrots, daikon, bamboo shoots, lotus root, taro root*, or kabocha pumpkin (can be left unpeeled) (either use one vegetable or as many kinds as desired)

Konnyaku (page 25), cut into large bite sized pieces (optional)

Fresh or reconstituted shiitake

Approximately 2 cups konbu broth (enough to barely cover the vegetables)

1 to 2 tablespoons sweetener of choice

1 to 3 tablespoons mirin

2 to 4 tablespoons soy sauce

Place the vegetable pieces and shiitake in a pot, and pour the broth over to barely cover. Add the sweetener and mirin, partially cover, and simmer until tender. Add the soy sauce and simmer for another 5 or 6 minutes. If desired, more seasonings can be added. The vegetables should be tender, not crisp (with the exception of lotus root which does not become really soft). Place the vegetables and broth attractively in individual bowls or a serving dish. Serve either hot or at room temperature.

This is more of a method for cooking vegetables, particularly root vegetables, than a particular recipe. A single vegetable such as carrots or lotus root can be used, or several can be used to prepare a dish known as inaka-ni (country-style stewed vegetables). Root vegetables, shiitake, and sometimes konnyaku are cut into large bite-sized pieces and simmered in a broth laced with soy sauce, sugar, and mirin. Thus, the method employed will be introduced here, and quantities suggested, but feel free to use more or less as desired.

Yield: 4 to 6 servings

*If using taro root, first parboil it for 5 minutes, then peel.

Braised Burdock Root

Kimpira-Gobo

Burdock root, an unusual but truly tasty vegetable, is the star of this dish. It is long, skinny, and covered with a hairy brown skin. Its high fiber content and crunchy texture make it a delicious and nutritious addition here. In this dish, it is braised with carrots and tossed with sesame seeds.

*To toast sesame seeds, heat the seeds in a small frying pan over medium heat until they make a crackling sound. Immediately remove from the heat.

2 large burdock roots, peeled and cut into matchsticks about 1 to 1½ inches long (approximately 4 cups)

1 tablespoon oil

2 medium carrots, scrubbed or peeled and cut into matchsticks about 1 to 1½ inches long (approximately 2 cups)

¼ cup *Konbu Dashi* (konbu stock), page 54 or water

3 tablespoons soy sauce

3 tablespoons mirin

1 tablespoon sweetener of choice (optional)

2 tablespoons toasted sesame seeds*

Yield: 3 to 6 servings

Burdock root discolors rapidly when cut due to oxygenation. To prevent this, or remove any discoloration, soak the cut pieces in water until you are ready to cook them. Drain well before cooking.

Heat the oil in a large sauté pan. Add the burdock root and sauté for 5 minutes. Add the carrots and continue to sauté for another 5 to 6 minutes. Add the stock or water, soy sauce, and mirin, and sweetener, and simmer over low heat, stirring occasionally, until all the liquid is absorbed and the vegetables are fairly tender. Toss with the toasted sesame seeds.

Spicy Braised Yam Cake
Konnyaku no Itame-Mono

1 konnyaku cake, page 25 (can be found in the
refrigerated section of Japanese stores)

1 tablespoon sesame oil

⅓ cup *Konbu Dashi* (konbu stock), page 54
or water

2 to 3 tablespoons soy sauce

About 2 dashes *shichimi* (Japanese 7-pepper spice)

Drain the konnyaku and rinse in fresh water.
Slice in half lengthwise, then in ¼-inch slices.
Heat the sesame oil in a skillet. Sauté the yam
cake slices for 3 to 4 minutes. Add the stock, soy
sauce, and shichimi, and simmer gently, stirring
occasionally, until almost all the liquid has evaporated. This can be served either hot or at room
temperature.

*Konnyaku is a grey or white
hard, rubbery looking food that
will most likely appear strange
to those new to it. It is made
from the root of a wild
mountain yam that is reportedly
calorie-free. (Really; I've checked
the nutrient content on this in
Japanese nutritional analysis
books.) I love it, although for
some people it may take some
getting used to. This is the way
my mother frequently
prepares it.*

Yield: 4 small servings

This simple, homey dish is one of my favorites.

Stewed Japanese Pumpkin
Kabocha no Ni-Mono

½ medium kabocha pumpkin, seeds and fiber removed

1 cup *Konbu Dashi* (Konbu Stock), page 54

¼ cup soy sauce

¼ cup mirin

1 to 2 tablespoons rice syrup, or FruitSource

With a very sharp knife, cut the kabocha into large chunks. Place all the ingredients in a heavy pot with a tight fitting lid, and bring to a boil. Reduce the heat to medium low, and simmer for about 15 minutes, or until the pumpkin is very tender and has absorbed the flavors. Serve hot or at room temperature.

Yield: 4 servings

Sesame Potatoes

Jagaimo no Goma-Ae

10 to 12 small red or new potatoes, halved or
    quartered

¼ cup sesame seeds

2 tablespoons soy sauce

2 tablespoons mirin

½ teaspoon sesame oil

In a pot with a tight fitting lid, cook the potatoes
with enough water to barely cover until tender.
Drain off the water.

In a heavy skillet over medium heat, toast the
sesame seeds until they make a slight crackling
sound and are light brown. (Jiggle the pan continuously.) Immediately add the soy sauce,
mirin, and sesame oil, and toss with the potatoes. Serve hot or at room temperature.

Yield: 4 servings

This is a classic example of a wonderful Japanese dish that is made with the simplest and fewest ingredients, and yet succeeds in celebrating the virtue of a particular vegetable. Thick rounds of daikon radish are simmered for a couple of hours in the milky water from washing white rice. This renders them tender to the point of practically melting in your mouth. The rounds are topped with dengaku, a sweet miso sauce that is featured in other dishes as well. This is definitely cold weather food.

Yield: 6 servings

Stewed Daikon with Sweet Miso Sauce

Furofuki Daikon

¾ to 1 whole, very thick, foot-long daikon (Skinny daikon will not do.)

Water from rinsing white rice (Oh, well, it won't hurt to have white rice once in a while!)

Cut the daikon into 2-inch-thick rings. With a sharp paring knife, peel each ring. Place in a pot and cover completely with the milky white water from the first rinsing of white rice. (This is most convenient if you will be cooking rice for dinner too). Cover tightly and simmer gently for 1½ to 2 hours. (The fatter the daikon, the longer you will want to cook it.) When the daikon rings are absolutely tender, remove and place in individual serving dishes. Top with *Miso Dengaku* (Sweet Miso Sauce, next page) and serve immediately.

Sweet Miso Sauce

Miso Dengaku

⅓ cup mild white or light brown miso (not dark red or dark brown)

¼ cup FruitSource, evaporated cane juice, or sugar

1 tablespoon sake

¾ cup *Konbu Dashi* (Konbu Stock), page 54 or water

Combine all the ingredients and stir. If using evaporated cane juice, I recommend that you combine it with the stock or water and heat it briefly to dissolve it first before combining with the other ingredients.

Yield: about 1¼ cups

The tops of daikon radishes are quite tasty and nutrient-rich if you are lucky enough to find them—perhaps at a farmers' market or Asian grocery store.

Braised Daikon Greens with Aburage

Abura-age to Daikon no Happa no Jtamemono

1 tablespoon sesame or canola oil

Approximately 3 cups thinly sliced daikon greens (a healthy bunch from 1 daikon)

2 pieces *abura-age* (fried tofu pouches), thinly sliced

⅓ cup *dashi* (stock)

1 to 2 tablespoons soy sauce

1 tablespoon sake

Heat the oil in a skillet. Add the daikon greens and sauté for 1 to 2 minutes. Add the *abura-age* (fried tofu pouches), and continue to sauté. When it begins to stick to the pan, add the *dashi* (stock), soy sauce, and sake, and simmer for a few minutes until tender.

Yield: 4 servings

Stewed Okara with Vegetables

U-no-hana

1½ cups *dashi* (stock)

¼ cup or more soy sauce

3 tablespoons mirin

1 tablespoon sake

2 teaspoons brown rice syrup, FruitSource, maple syrup, evaporated cane juice, or sugar

1 tablespoon oil

½ leek, or 1 bunch scallions, thinly sliced

3 cups packed okara

1 cup green peas

5 to 6 dried shiitake, reconstituted and thinly sliced

1 carrot, cut into matchsticks ½ inch long

1 piece *abura-age* (fried tofu pouches), thinly sliced

Okara, the fluffy white by-product of tofu production, is largely used to feed livestock. If you ever end up with any from making your own soymilk or tofu, or are able to procure it from a tofu manufacturer or Japanese grocer, try making this traditional Japanese country-style dish.

Combine the *dashi* (stock) with the soy sauce, mirin, sake, and sweetener. Set aside. Heat the oil in a large skillet. Add the leek and sauté momentarily. Add the okara, shiitake, carrot, *abura-age* (fried tofu pouches), and the *dashi* (stock) mixture, and stir well. Simmer for 20 minutes, stirring occasionally.

The flavors should be well combined. Most of the liquid will evaporate so that the okara will have about the same moisture level as it did at the start. Add more soy sauce or mirin to taste. (It should be savory with a touch of sweetness).

Yield: 4 to 6 servings

133

A simple appetizer popular in Japanese drinking establishments, delicate enoki mushrooms are baked with a sprinkling of sake or white wine, and traditionally, butter. I have substituted extra-virgin olive oil. A dry sake is preferable to a sweeter one for this dish.

Enoki Mushrooms with Sake or White Wine

Enoki no Saka-Mushi (or) Enoki no Shiro-Wine Mushi

3½ ounces enoki mushrooms
2 teaspoons extra-virgin olive oil
2 tablespoons dry sake or white wine
Salt, to taste

Preheat the oven to 375°F.

Trim the bottom ½ inch off the enoki mushrooms. Break into 2 or 3 clumps, and place in a small baking dish. Drizzle on the olive oil and sake, and sprinkle with salt. Cover with a lid or a piece of aluminum foil, and bake for 10 to 15 minutes.

Yield: 2 servings

Meals in a Bowl
Donburi

Donburi covers a class of filling, homey dishes that are all constructed in large, individual bowls. (*Donburi* means bowl.) Colorfully decorated bowls are filled with rice and topped with a range of savory toppings. They constitute a one-bowl meal accompanied by a smaller bowl of miso soup and are generally very simple to make. Many classic dishes have a donburi counterpart—sukiyaki can top a donburi of rice to form *sukiyaki-donburi*, or tempura can be transformed into *tendon*. Even raw tuna can top rice to become *tekka-don*. (Of course there is no vegetarian counterpart to this one!) One of the most famous is *oyako-donburi*, which means "parent and child" donburi. It is made with chicken and egg. In this chapter, I've replicated it with a delicious vegan version and present it along with a few other interesting bowls of rice.

Rice Bowl Topped with Tempura

Tendon

For each Donburi (bowl):

Fill each bowl about three-quarters full with hot rice. Place several pieces of hot tempura and tempura pieces with 3 to 4 tablespoons of slightly concentrated *ten-tsuyu* (tempura sauce), page 90. (To concentrate tempura sauce, boil rapidly for a few minutes.) The sauce will seep through the tempura pieces and drip down into the rice, seasoning it along with the tempura. Serve immediately.

The simple act of piling tempura on a bowl of steaming rice and dousing it with ten-tsuyu (tempura sauce) transforms tempura into a different dish. The rice becomes delectably seasoned, and with each bite you can enjoy that perfect marriage of components that donburi dishes promise. This is the answer to any leftover tempura you might have. (Leftovers should be reheated in an oven to regain their crispy coating; microwaving will render them soft and mushy.)

This may be a good introduction to those who have not yet tried natto, since the slightly slimy beans become quite savory here.

Natto-Donburi

5 to 6 ounces natto (2 regular or 3 small packs)

1 tablespoon oil

¼ to ⅕ head small cabbage, diced into ½-inch pieces (about 4 to 5 cups)

1 carrot, cut in half and thinly sliced

4 to 5 shiitake mushrooms, reconstituted and thinly sliced (optional)

1 piece *abura-age* (fried tofu pouch), thinly sliced

1 cup *dashi* (stock)

3 tablespoons mirin

4 tablespoons soy sauce

1 tablespoon cornstarch

¼ cup more *dashi* (stock) or water

1 bunch scallions

1 teaspoon sesame oil

6 cups hot rice, either brown or white

Karashi (little packets of mustard that may come with the natto) (optional)

Yield: 3 servings

Place the natto in a small colander, and rinse under running water, stirring with a pair of chopsticks to rid it of most of its sliminess. Drain. Heat 1 tablespoon of oil in a skillet or wok. Sauté the cabbage, carrot, and shiitake until crisp-tender. Add the abura-age, natto, 1 cup of dashi, mirin, and soy sauce, and simmer gently for a few minutes to heat through. Dissolve the cornstarch in the additional ¼ cup

of dashi or water, and add to the mixture in the pan. Stir until it thickens into a thin glaze. Add the scallions, stir for a minute to combine, then add the teaspoon of sesame oil. Turn off the heat. Divide the rice into 3 *donburis* (large, deep bowls. Top with the mixture and serve immediately. If desired, you can add a little karashi to your bowl.

The direct translation of this dish, "Rice Bowl of Parent and Child," does not sound particularly appetizing, in my book. It refers to a dish where chicken pieces have been scrambled with eggs and served on top of rice. This description doesn't do it for me, but it happens to be a favorite dish of the Japanese, as well as one of mine once many, many moons ago. Recently, I was able to replicate it with chicken-flavored seitan and puréed tofu. It is simple to make and quite tasty.

Yield: 3 servings

Rice Bowl with "Chicken" and "Egg"

Oyako Donburi

1½ to 2 cups *dashi* (stock)

4 tablespoons soy sauce

3 tablespoons mirin

1 tablespoon sweetener of your choice, such as evaporated cane juice, FruitSource, maple syrup, or brown rice syrup

1 onion, sliced

8 ounces seitan "chicken" pieces

8 ounces silken tofu

5 tablespoons cornstarch or arrowroot

Dash of turmeric for color (optional)

5 to 6 cups cooked hot rice

Place the *dashi* (stock), soy sauce, mirin, sweetener, and onion in a skillet, and simmer gently over medium-low heat for about 5 minutes. Add the seitan pieces and continue to simmer gently, stirring occasionally, until the onions are very tender. There should still be enough liquid in the pan to come up part way on the seitan. Purée the tofu, cornstarch, and turmeric in a blender until smooth. Pour into the simmering mixture, but do not stir. Swish the pan around a bit to allow some of the liquid to come over the tofu.

Cover the pan and simmer until the tofu is firm to the touch, about 7 minutes. There should still be sauce in the pan.

Divide the rice into 3 *donburi* (large, deep bowls). Lift out the mixture with a spatula and top each bowl with some. Pour any additional sauce on top.

This is an original vegan recipe created to replicate what was once one of my favorite dishes.

Yield: 4 servings

Vegetarian Eel over Rice
Unaju or Unagi Donburi

10 dried shiitake, reconstituted
½ cup reconstituted wakame
1 packed cup reconstituted yuba
2 tablespoons soy sauce
1 tablespoon mirin
3 tablespoons *mochiko* (glutinous rice flour)
4 sheets nori
2 tablespoons oil
Tare Sauce (see recipe next page)
4 cups hot white or brown rice

Place the shiitake and wakame in a food processor, and process until finely minced. Shred the yuba into small pieces. Mix the yuba with the wakame mixture, and season with the soy sauce and mirin. Mix in the *mochiko* (rice flour). Divide this mixture into fourths, and place a mound on each sheet of nori. Pat it out into a rectangle, and fold the nori over the mixture to form a packet, sealing the nori with water to make it stick. Heat the oil in a frying pan, and sauté the "eel" on both sides until crispy. Add 3 to 4 tablespoons of the tare sauce to the pan, and flip the "eel" over a couple of times to allow the sauce to penetrate. Place hot rice in individual

bowls, place a piece of "eel" on top of each, and pour 2 to 3 tablespoons of tare over each piece again, this time allowing the sauce to flavor the rice. Serve immediately.

Tare Sauce for "Eel"

⅓ cup evaporated cane juice

½ cup *Konbu Dashi* (Konbu Stock), page 54

½ cup soy sauce

3 tablespoons mirin

Combine and simmer all the ingredients for 5 to 10 minutes, or until the mixture forms a thin syrup. This keeps well.

Yield: 6 to 8 servings

Everyday Favorites

The dishes in this chapter are familiar favorites in most homes. These are not centuries-old dishes, but rather more recent adaptations of Western-style dishes to suit the Japanese palate. They use ingredients and cooking techniques which were not used by the Japanese until the 20th century, and many reflect the recent practice of eating meat. (Of course, the recipes presented here are vegetarian versions, although you might not find such in Japan!) These are the everyday dishes that Japanese housewives stand by, since they are so popular with children; they are, in essence, the Japanese equivalents of American pizza or macaroni and cheese. But believe me, their homey flavors will be enjoyed by adults as well.

Savory Vegetable Pancakes

Okonomiyaki

2 cups water

¼ pound regular tofu

2½ cups whole wheat pastry or unbleached white flour

1 teaspoon salt

2 teaspoons baking powder

4 to 5 cups thinly sliced or slivered vegetables: onions, carrot matchsticks, cabbage, broccoli, green beans, mushrooms, etc.

Purée the water and tofu in a blender until smooth. Combine the flour, salt, and baking powder in a large bowl, and mix well. Pour in the liquid mixture, and mix lightly. Add the vegetables and mix well to combine.

Cook large pancakes on a lightly oiled skillet or griddle over medium-low heat until browned on both sides. Serve while hot with soy sauce or *tonkatsu* sauce (see *sosu* page 32).

("Sauce" is served with a variety of other foods, mostly fried. I find this more healthful vegan version is delicious with just soy sauce, although kids prefer the tasty "sauce.")

This literally translates into "favorite grilled food." In Japan, these huge, tempting pancakes filled with vegetables and seafood (usually octopus and squid) are sold at street fairs from stands as well as at specialty restaurants where they are grilled at your table in front of your very eyes. The restaurant may also provide the batter and "fixings" for you to grill them yourself on the built-in table grill. They are generally smothered in what the Japanese refer to as "sauce," a thick, brown concoction that tastes like Worcestershire sauce. By the way, this is another way I can get my little boy to devour his vegetables!

Yield: 4 to 6 servings

Curry rice is cult food in Japan. Typically, a housewife will procure a box of "curry roux" at the grocery store, a solid block of curry, flavorings, flour, and oil or fat, that cooks up into a thick, creamy sauce when stewed with meat, vegetables, and water. I don't know when curry was introduced into Japan, but it has worked its magic over the entire nation. Not only does almost every restaurant serve curry rice, but there are specialty restaurants that serve nothing else and magazine features on how to make the best curry.

Yield: 6 servings

Curry Rice

Karei Rice

2 tablespoons oil

2 large onions, sliced

2 cloves garlic, minced

2 to 6 tablespoons curry powder, depending on how hot you like it and the strength of the curry powder (Use the smaller amount if you are serving children.)

½ to ⅔ cup flour

3 cups hot, beef-style vegetarian stock (homemade or from cubes or powder)

1 apple, peeled and grated in a fine pulp

3 to 4 tablespoons soy sauce

2 tablespoons evaporated cane juice, fruit juice concentrate, FruitSource, or 3 to 4 tablespoons frozen apple juice concentrate

2 cups cubed potatoes (preferably red)

2 carrots, cut into ¼-inch slices

Meat substitute of your choice (optional), such as:

1 cup textured soy protein chunks or strips, reconstituted in boiling water to cover and drained,

1 cup chopped seitan

One 12-ounce package extra-firm tofu, cut into cubes,

5 or 6 vegetarian hot dogs, sliced

½ cup rich soymilk

1 cup broccoli florets or string beans (Another green vegetable may be substituted.)

1 cup frozen corn (optional)

Heat the oil in a heavy-bottomed 3-quart saucepan. Add the onions and garlic, cover, and sauté, stirring occasionally, until the onions are translucent and soft. Add the curry powder and sauté for a couple of minutes. Add the flour (the greater amount for a thicker sauce), and cook for another 2 minutes. Pour in the stock and whisk or beat with a wooden spoon until smooth. Add the apple, soy sauce, sweetener of choice, potatoes, carrots, and meat substitute of choice; cover and simmer for 15 minutes. Add the soymilk, broccoli, and corn, and cook for another 10 minutes or so until tender. Add more soy sauce, curry, or vegetable broth powder to taste. To serve, pour next to a generous mound of rice on a plate. Let people eat with spoons if they want!

There are some restaurants that let you order the degree of hotness from 1 to 10 (and will not charge you for the meal if you can eat the 10 degree concoction!), but the most common version is rather mild and enjoyed greatly by children. I remember loving it as a child, as my children do now . Of course, the recipe presented here does not come from a box , but is a more healthful version made "from scratch." For a most authentic taste, use curry powder made by a Japanese manufacturer. (It usually comes in a small can and can be found at Japanese grocery stores.)

This is a Japanese adaptation of a Chinese favorite. You can find vital wheat gluten in health food stores; it is pure powdered wheat protein used in bread baking and by vegetarians both in Asia and in the West to make vegetarian meat substitutes.

Yield: 4 to 8 servings

Japanese Potstickers

Gyoza

¼ medium cabbage, shredded

1 cup textured soy protein granules

1 cup boiling water

1 clove garlic, minced

1 teaspoon grated fresh ginger

2 tablespoons soy sauce

½ cup vital wheat gluten

2 teaspoons toasted sesame oil

5 dried shiitake, reconstituted and chopped

½ cup thinly sliced green onions

Oil or nonstick spray for cooking

25 to 30 potsticker skins (available in Asian and many regular supermarkets)

Sauté the cabbage in a little water until tender. Reconstitute the soy protein granules with the boiling water for 10 minutes. Add the garlic, ginger, and soy sauce, and mix well. Add the vital wheat gluten and mix well. Add the sesame oil, shiitake, green onions, and cabbage, and combine well. Adjust the seasonings to taste.

Make sure that your hands are very clean and dry before starting to assemble the potstickers. Place a mounded teaspoon or so of the mixture in the center of a potsticker skin. (The amount will depend on the size of the wrappers; some are bigger than others.) Fold the skin over so that the edges meet. Dip a finger in some water, and run it along one of the inner edges of the skin so that the edges stick together. Then crimp the edges together (see illustration). Place on a plate or cookie sheet that has been lightly dusted with cornstarch. Continue with the remaining skins.

To cook, heat a small amount of oil, or use a nonstick cooking spray in a nonstick pan. When the pan is hot, place the *gyoza* (potstickers) in the pan in neat rows. (This will make it easier for flipping.) Over medium heat, cook on one side until nicely browned. Flip over, pour 3 to 4 tablespoons of water into the pan, and place a lid over the pan. Allow to cook for another couple of minutes until most of the water has evaporated and the potstickers are glistening. Serve with soy sauce, a dash of hot chili oil, if you have some on hand, and a dash of rice vinegar.

Here is another excellent way to get your kids to eat their vegetables—mine will ask for seconds and thirds. "Ko-ro-keh," as they are pronounced in Japanese, are presumably a Japanese adaptation of French croquettes. They are generally potato-based with creamy bechamel sauce as a binder and are laced with ground meat, seafood, or vegetables. This more healthful version is just as satisfying. For those who want to avoid deep frying, they can be baked at a high temperature to yield similar results.

Yield: 6 servings

Vegetable Croquettes

Yasai Korrokeh

1½ pounds well-scrubbed potatoes

⅓ cup soymilk

2 carrots, diced small and steamed briefly until tender-crisp

½ to ¾ cup fresh or frozen green peas

½ to ¾ cup fresh or frozen corn

1 tablespoon soy sauce

Salt and pepper, to taste

Flour for coating

1 cup soymilk for dipping

2 cups *panko* (dry bread crumbs)

Oil for deep frying or nonstick cooking spray

½ cup ketchup

3 tablespoons soy sauce

Place the potatoes in a pot with water to cover, and bring to a boil. Turn down the heat and cook until tender. Allow to cool before handling, then slip the skins off. Place half the potatoes in a food processor, and process for a minute until smooth. The resulting mixture should be slightly elastic. (This helps it to bind together.) Mash the remaining potatoes in a bowl, and combine with the soymilk and processed potatoes. Mix in the vegetables and flavor with the 1 tablespoon

soy sauce, salt, and pepper. Form 10 to 12 small croquettes about ⅓ to ½ inch thick. Coat each croquette with flour, dip in the soymilk, and coat well with the bread crumbs.

To cook, either use the traditional method of deep-frying until golden brown, or place on a baking sheet that has been sprayed with a non-stick cooking spray, spray the croquettes well, and then bake for 15 to 20 minutes at 400°F until crispy and brown. Serve with *tonkatsu sauce* (see *sosu* page 32) or combine the ketchup and 3 tablespoons soy sauce for a croquette sauce.

Croquettes are generally served with the ubiquitous tonkatsu sauce, but I like to serve them with the simple ketchup-soy sauce mixture in this recipe. The potatoes can be cooked hours or a day ahead if desired.

Croquettes with Ground "Beef"

Niku-Korrokeh

Prepare as for Vegetable Croquettes, but instead of the carrots, corn, and peas, add:

½ cup textured soy protein granules reconstituted with ¼ cup boiling water, plus 2 tablespoons soy sauce and 1 teaspoon sesame oil,

or the equivalent of any other type of meat substitute, such as "ground beef" or "sausage"

151

Topped with the ubiquitous bottled tonkatsu sauce, a large heap of refreshing shredded raw cabbage (upon which the same brown sauce is poured), and a bowl of rice, a simply prepared hearty meal is ready.

Vegetarian "Pork"

2 cups water

3 tablespoons soy sauce or Bragg Liquid Aminos

3 cloves garlic, minced

3 tablespoons nutritional yeast

Dash of black or white pepper

2 cups vital wheat gluten

Oil for sautéing

Flour for coating

1 cup soymilk for dipping

2 cups *panko* (dry bread crumbs)

Oil for deep frying or nonstick cooking spray

Combine the water with the soy sauce, garlic, nutritional yeast, and pepper. Mix in the vital wheat gluten; the mixture should be very soft. Divide this into 6 to 8 pieces, and pat out into "steak"-shaped pieces about ½-inch thick. Heat a little oil in a skillet (preferably nonstick), and fry the pieces until browned and crispy on both sides. Transfer the pieces to a pot of boiling water, and simmer for 20 to 30 minutes, or until tender. Drain the simmering liquid. (The resulting stock makes a good base for soup.)

Coat each piece of cooked gluten (seitan) in the flour, dip in the soymilk, then in the *panko* (dried breadcrumbs), and deep-fry until golden brown. Serve with *tonkatsu* sauce (see *sosu* page 32).

Deep-Fried Pork, Vegan-Style
Tonkatsu

1 recipe Vegetarian "Pork," facing page

Flour for dredging

1 to 1½ to cups soymilk

3 to 4 cups *panko* (Japanese crispy, dry bread crumbs used for deep-frying), or homemade fine breadcrumbs

Oil for deep-frying

Tonkatsu sauce (a thick, Worcestershire-type sauce made from vegetables, fruit, sugar, and salt, available in Japanese food stores)

The Japanese are proud of their salmonella-free pork that can be served medium rare as a breaded and deep-fried popular specialty called tonkatsu. Of course, this is not anything I'm proud of. In fact, pork chops were the last piece of meat my mother put before me when I became a vegetarian. (I refused to eat them, seeing a dead pig, of course.) However, Tenmi, a natural food restaurant in Tokyo that I frequented, served a vegan version of this using kofu (wheat gluten) that provided my vegetarian palate with the same sense of rich satisfaction that the meat counterpart gives most Japanese.

Dredge each piece of the cooked seitan in the flour. Dip in the soymilk, then dredge in the breadcrumbs to coat thoroughly. Heat the oil in a fryer or wok until a small piece of the seitan dropped into it rises quickly to the top. Fry the breaded slices in the oil until golden brown on both sides; it will be necessary to turn them over after a couple of minutes. Remove to drain on paper towels several layers thick or on brown paper. Slice each piece into 1-inch wide sections. Ideally, place on a plate next to a large heap of very finely shredded raw cabbage. Serve while hot topped with tonkatsu sauce.

Fermented Soy Beans

Natto

"Can you eat natto?" is a question a Japanese will often pose to test a foreigner who seems intrepid in his relentless quest to conquer things Japanese. And all too often, even the foreigner who is conversant in Japanese, has a black belt in karate, and has mastered the art of bowing, may admit that he, however, cannot stomach natto. Clearly, I have not provided a very good introduction to one of my favorite foods. However, if ever a food can be described as an acquired taste, I suppose natto may lead the pack. With a distinct smell some liken to a strong cheese and a sticky, slightly slimy texture, many who are introduced to it in adulthood find they have no taste for it.

Still, a hardcore following of natto lovers enjoy it prepared in numerous ways, but most often poured over a bowl of steaming hot rice. For some reason, young children seem to love it; for all three of mine, it was love at first bite, and they will eat it out of the package today. And of course, there are those foreigners who smile broadly when asked the question and reply, "*Dai-suki desu!*" ("I love it!").

Natto is served either cold or at room temperature over hot rice. It is also great in hand-rolled sushi, especially with a leaf of shiso. Packed with nutrition, digestive enzymes, and "friendly" bacteria, it takes only a few seconds to prepare and makes an excellent instant meal over rice. Natto made from small beans is tastier and more tender than that made from large beans; ask the store owner if you cannot read the Japanese on the package. Also, there is a natto called *hiki-wari* or minced natto that is also excellent.

Natto

One 3-ounce package natto
1 teaspoon soy sauce
½ teaspoon Japanese mustard paste (optional)
1 to 2 scallions, chopped (optional)

Mix the natto with the soy sauce and mustard, then mix in the scallions. It will get stretchy and form "threads." Serve over hot rice.

Yield: 1 to 2 servings

155

Mushroom Doria

On a typical "café" lunch menu in Japan, one will often encounter dishes such as rice pilaf, gratin, and sandwiches, all Japanese adaptations of Western dishes. In addition to these, a dish called *doria* frequently appears. I am not sure what the origins of this seemingly Western dish is, although I suspect that it is genuinely Japanese. Many Japanese, however, think it is an American dish, although I have yet to meet an American who has heard of a *doria*. I suspect it has roots similar to chop suey, a seemingly Chinese dish that was supposedly invented in San Francisco. A *doria* is a gratin of rice covered with vegetables, seafood, or meat in bèchamel (white sauce). It actually makes a tasty combination, despite the suspicious origins.

With a tasty white sauce (made with a rich soymilk, of course), almost anything can be thrown into a doria. Although I have used a combination of mushrooms here (accented by some baby spinach) a variety of other vegetables such as asparagus, peas, broccoli, carrots, and tasty meat alternatives, such as slices of tofu hot dogs or bits of vegetarian sausage, can be substituted. Armed with the following recipe for a tasty white sauce, the doria is a loosely knit recipe that can be adapted in a variety of ways befitting the ingredients on hand. It also presents a wonderful opportunity to recycle leftover cooked vegetables and rice and transform them into a creative one-dish meal.

Mushroom Doria

Thick Bèchamel (White Sauce)

3 tablespoons canola oil

½ onion, chopped

7 tablespoons flour (preferably all-purpose unbleached)

2 cups hot soymilk (Vitasoy Creamy Original is recommended)

Salt, to taste

1 to 2 dashes white pepper

Several pinches freshly grated nutmeg

2 tablespoons white wine (optional)

Heat the oil in a heavy-bottomed saucepan. Add the onion, lower the heat, and cover. Cook, stirring occasionally, until the onion is soft. Add the flour and stir with a wooden spoon until the flour turns white. Whisk in the hot soymilk all at once. You will find that using a hot liquid will thicken the sauce almost immediately and will not form lumps. If you have forgotten to heat your soymilk, add it slowly in a steady stream, whisking continuously; otherwise, it will form lumps. Cook until thickened, stirring almost constantly. Season with salt, white pepper, several gratings of fresh nutmeg, and the white wine, if desired.

To make the Doria:

1 pound mushrooms, a mixture of 8 ounces
   button or crimini mushrooms, quartered,
   4 ounces shiitake mushrooms, sliced,
   and 4 ounces oyster mushrooms, torn
   by hand into individual mushrooms,
   or 1 pound button mushrooms, quartered

2 cups loosely packed baby spinach leaves

1 to 2 tablespoons oil or cooking spray

Salt and pepper, to taste

Approximately 4 cups cooked short-grain white or
   brown rice, warm or hot

Heat the oil over high heat (preferably in a non-stick pan), and add the mushrooms so that there is no more than one layer in the pan. Cook them on high heat, tossing or stirring them, until they brown. (Crowding them will make them watery and not brown.) Season with salt and pepper. Repeat with the remaining mushrooms, if necessary, depending on the size of your pan. Before you remove the last bunch of mushrooms from your pan, add the spinach and cook momentarily, only allowing it to wilt. Combine the mushrooms and spinach with the bèchamel sauce. Distribute the rice into four oiled gratin or small casserole dishes. Top with the mushroom and sauce mixture.

Place in a preheated 400°F oven, and bake for about 15 to 20 minutes, or until the sauce is bubbly and hot. If desired, sprinkle a few bread-crumbs on top, and stick under the broiler to brown. Serve immediately.

Yield: 4 servings

"Meat" and Potatoes
Niku-Jaga

1 to 1½ cups textured soy protein granules

1 to 1½ cups boiling water

2 to 3 large potatoes, peeled or scrubbed well and cut into large 1- to 1½-inch chunks

2 carrots, cut into 1-inch circles (optional)

1 cup water for cooking

4 to 5 tablespoons soy sauce

3 tablespoons mirin

2 tablespoons sweetener of your choice

3 cloves garlic, minced

1 tablespoon nutritional yeast (optional)

Soak the soy protein granules in the boiling water to reconstitute for 10 minutes. Place the potatoes, carrots, and 1 cup water in a pot, cover, and cook for 5 minutes. Add the reconstituted soy granules and the seasonings, partially cover, and simmer until the potatoes and carrots are tender and most of the liquid has evaporated. Adjust the seasonings to taste. Serve hot.

Textured soy protein is employed here to create a vegan version of a popular dish where ground beef and potatoes are cooked together with slightly sweet and savory seasonings. This is popular with both kids and adults.

Yield: 4 to 6 servings

Nouvelle Japanese Cuisine

The Japanese are famous for their ability to adapt to or accept input from other cultures. Although they may not consider themselves a highly original people, the Japanese are very good at incorporating just about anything from other countries and cultures and adapting, emulating, and improving upon them. This extends to food as well. Tokyo thus abounds with ethnic restaurants—not only those that cater to Chinese and Italian cuisines which are so popular world-wide, but also highly sophisticated French or French-influenced cuisine. The most remarkable restaurants are those where creative Japanese chefs have borrowed from the traditions and techniques of other cultures, married them with their own cuisine and ingredients, and produced something entirely new. This, I call "nouvelle Japanese," and here I happily introduce a few simple recipes that replicate some of the flavors I have tasted at some of these eateries.

Pasta with Shiso Pesto

Supageti to Shiso no Basilico Sauce

10 bunches shiso (100 leaves; there are usually 10 leaves to a bunch)

1 cup extra-virgin olive oil

2 to 3 cloves garlic

¼ cup pine nuts

2 to 3 tablespoons mild miso

2 teaspoons *ume* (salted plum paste) (optional)

Pasta of choice, cooked al dente

Place all the ingredients, except the pasta, in a blender, and blend until finely chopped or until smooth, whichever you prefer. Toss with hot, drained pasta, and serve immediately.

Shiso is a fragrant Japanese herb which is sometimes referred to as Japanese basil. Its large, beautiful leaves make an appearance in a variety of Japanese dishes, often paired with ume (salted plum), but it lends itself beautifully to a pesto sauce. If you are lucky enough to find yourself with a big harvest of shiso leaves (it is actually quite easy to grow yourself), here is what to do with some of it.

This makes enough sauce for about a pound of pasta, enough to serve about eight people. Leftover sauce can be refrigerated for two to three weeks or frozen.

Yield: 8 servings

Mushroom lovers will appreciate this flavorful dish abounding with three kinds of mushrooms in a fragrant broth with a hint of shiso and topped with slivers of nori.

With this dish, it is best not to make more than 2 servings at a time.

Yield: 1 serving

Spaghetti with Mushrooms
Kinoko Spaghetti

Have ready:

1 cup cooked spaghetti, vermicelli, or angel hair pasta, cooked al dente

1 teaspoon sesame oil

2 fresh shiitake mushrooms, sliced

2 enoki mushrooms, separated

2 *shimeji* or regular oyster mushrooms, separated

1 tablespoon sake

1 tablespoon white wine

⅓ cup *Konbu to Shiitake no Dashi* (Shiitake Stock), page 54

1 tablespoon mirin

2 tablespoons soy sauce

1 teaspoon sesame oil

4 to 5 shiso leaves, slivered (stack them, roll them, and sliver with a sharp knife or pair of scissors)

1/2 piece nori, slivered (cut in half, stack, and cut in slivers with a pair of scissors)

Heat 1 teaspoon sesame oil in a sauté pan, and sauté the mushrooms over high heat until they wilt slightly. Deglaze the pan by pouring in the sake and white wine, then add the shiitake stock, mirin, and soy sauce. Bring to a simmer and cook for 2 to 3 minutes, then toss in the cooked pasta, and heat for 30 seconds. Turn off the heat, add the sesame oil and shiso, and put into individual bowls. Top with a mound of slivered nori. Consume immediately.

Steamed Kabocha with Lemon Crème Fraîche

Kabocha no Lemon Kureem Kake

½ medium-size kabocha, unpeeled, either sliced into ¼-inch slices or cut into large chunks (the latter is for mashing)

Steam the kabocha until tender. If you are serving slices, place the unpeeled slices on individual plates. If you are mashing, scoop the orange meat out, and discard the skin. Mash with a whisk, seasoning lightly with salt and pepper if desired. Place a mound of kabocha in small, individual dishes. For either method, top the kabocha with Lemon Crème Fraîche, and serve.

Lemon Crème Fraîche

5 to 6 ounces firm silken tofu (½ of an aseptic package)

3 tablespoons lemon juice

3 tablespoons water

2 tablespoons salad oil

½ teaspoon salt

2 tablespoons fructose, sugar, FruitSource, or fruit juice concentrate

Combine all the ingredients in a blender until absolutely smooth.

This very simple and unique dish is a vegan replication of something I tasted at a progressive nomi-ya (a Japanese drinking establishment serving a variety of tapas-style delectables). In the original version, heavy cream was used. I have substituted silken tofu with excellent results.

This can be served two ways; you can pour the crème fraîche over sliced, steamed kabocha, or you can mash and whip the kabocha and pour the crème over that. Served at room temperature, this can be either an appetizer or side dish.

Yield: 4 servings

163

This refreshing salad is excellent for summer, either as an appetizer or as a small side salad. The daikon wilts quickly, diluting the dressing and becoming "pickled" after only a few minutes, so toss with the dressing just before serving.

Yield: 4 to 6 servings

Daikon Salad with Lime-Ume Dressing

Daikon Salada

⅓ cup freshly squeezed lime juice

⅓ cup fructose, sugar, or FruitSource

1 tablespoon *ume* (salted ume plum paste) (Look for a brand without food coloring or additives.)

12 ounces daikon, peeled and cut into thin matchsticks

Red leaf or butter lettuce for garnishing

1 sheet nori, slivered (optional)*

Mix the lime juice, sweetener, and ume paste well. Combine with the daikon and toss. Place a mound of daikon on a lettuce leaf, top with nori slivers, and serve immediately.

*To sliver the nori, cut it into 4 long pieces, stack them together, and cut into thin short strips with a pair of scissors.

Mushroom Salad

Mashurumu to Shiso no Salada

Dressing

1 tablespoon soy sauce

⅓ cup balsamic vinegar

⅓ cup rice vinegar

3 tablespoons chopped garlic

Scant ½ cup extra-virgin olive oil

Dash cayenne

6 ounces enoki mushrooms

8 ounces *shimeji* (oyster mushrooms)

4 ounces button mushrooms

15 shiso leaves

This marinated salad can serve as an easy and delicious appetizer on a bed of greens. Alternatively, it can be an accompaniment to a meal.

To make the dressing, combine the soy sauce, vinegars, and garlic, then whisk in the olive oil in a steady stream. Add a dash of cayenne pepper, to taste.

Trim the bottom of the enoki mushroom clump, and separate into individual or small clumps of mushrooms. Trim the bottoms of the *shimeji* (oyster mushrooms), and separate into small sections by hand. Thinly slice the button mushrooms. Stack the shiso leaves, roll them up, then sliver with a sharp knife. Combine with the mushrooms in a bowl. Toss with the dressing and allow to marinate for 30 minutes before serving.

Instead of the typical dreary pasta salad, try taking this to your next picnic. You'll have everyone raving.

Yield: 3 to 6 servings, depending on whether it is served as a luncheon entrée or a picnic dish.

Soba Salad

Dressing

½ cup canola oil

2 tablespoons dark sesame oil

½ cup rice vinegar

2 tablespoons maple syrup or evaporated cane juice

8 ounces dry soba noodles

2 red bell peppers

1 bunch asparagus, 2 medium zucchini, or ½ head broccoli

10 fresh or dried and reconstituted shiitake mushrooms

2 tablespoons olive oil

Salt, to taste

2 ears of corn, preferably white (frozen may be used)

1 bunch scallions

1 Japanese cucumber, thinly sliced

¼ cup toasted sesame seeds

To make the dressing, combine all of the dressing ingredients in a jar, and shake well.

Cook the soba in boiling water until al dente. Drain and run under cold water until cold. Set aside.

Trim and cut the red bell pepper into strips, then cut them in half. Cut the asparagus into 1-inch lengths, or if using zucchini, slice into ¼-inch slices. For broccoli, separate into small florets. Trim the stems from the shiitake, and cut into either quarters or halves, depending on the size of the mushroom. Place the vegetables onto a sheet pan, and toss with the olive oil and salt, thoroughly coating each piece. Bake at 375°F for about 15 minutes, or until tender.

Cut the kernels off of the ears of corn, and slice the scallions thinly. Combine the cooked soba with the roasted vegetables, corn, and scallions. Combine with the dressing. Arrange the cucumber slices on top, and sprinkle with the sesame seeds.

Optional Method:

Simply use all the vegetables in their raw state, or blanch some of them briefly.

Although roasting the asparagus gives it a rich, savory flavor that contrasts nicely with the light, tangy ponzu (light citrus dipping sauce), it is also tasty served either steamed, blanched, or grilled.

When making the sauce, adjust the salt to taste according to the sweetener used. It should be tangy, but balanced with sweetness and saltiness.

Roasted Asparagus with Lime Ponzu Sauce

Lime Ponzu Sauce

¼ cup lime juice

1 tablespoon soy sauce

½ teaspoon salt

1 tablespoon sweetener of choice such as FruitSource, evaporated cane juice, maple syrup, or 2 tablespoons frozen concentrated fruit juice

2 to 3 tablespoons mirin

1 pound asparagus

1 to 2 tablespoons olive oil

Salt, to taste

2 teaspoons toasted sesame seeds

Combine all the ingredients for the sauce.

Preheat the oven to 400°F. Wash and trim the tough bottoms of the asparagus. Toss the asparagus with the olive oil, and sprinkle with salt to taste. Place on a baking sheet, and place in the oven for about 10 to 15 minutes (depending on the thickness), until the asparagus is tender-crisp, and quite tasty. Place a few stalks on each plate, pour on the Lime Ponzu Sauce, and sprinkle with the sesame seeds.

Index